Winston Churchill

www.pocketessentials.com

Other books by Bill Price in this series

Tutankhamun
Celtic Myths
Charles Darwin

Winston Churchill
War Leader

BILL PRICE

POCKET ESSENTIALS

First published in 2009 by Pocket Essentials
PO Box 394, Harpenden, Herts, AL5 1XJ
www.pocketessentials.com

A CIP catalogue record for this book is available from the British Library.

ISBN 978–1–84243–322–5

2 4 6 8 10 9 7 5 3 1

Typeset by Avocet Typeset, Chilton, Aylesbury, Bucks
Printed and bound in Great Britain by JF Print, Sparkford, Somerset

Contents

CONTENTS

Introduction

One of the pitfalls of biographical writing is a tendency to exaggerate the importance of the individual concerned at the expense of a wider appreciation of the times. But in the case of Winston Churchill such concerns are much less pronounced. He was at the centre of so many of the momentous events of the first half of the twentieth century that, rather than exaggerating his role, it actually becomes hard not to underestimate his contribution.

As a young man Churchill thought of himself as a 'man of destiny' and consciously set out to emulate his heroes, including his illustrious ancestor John Churchill, the first Duke of Marlborough. He embarked on a pre-determined plan to make his name through military exploits and then to enter politics, but his naked ambition and combative nature divided opinion from the beginning. Some considered him to be intuitively brilliant while to others he was always a dangerous opportunist.

In the 1930s, successive Conservative Prime Ministers considered Churchill too much of a liability to be trusted with a ministerial job, leading to a period on the backbenches now often described as his 'wilderness years'. Even before Adolf Hitler and the Nazi Party came to power in Germany, he was issuing warnings about the threat they posed to European peace and he campaigned against the British Government's policies of disarmament and appeasement. At the outbreak of the Second World War in September 1939 he was finally recalled to the Government, initially as First Lord of the Admiralty and then as Prime Minister, thereby achieving his lifelong ambition at one of the most difficult and dangerous moments in British history.

Since the end of the war, and particularly after his death, Churchill's role in the Second World War has been endlessly debated, with opinions about him remaining as divided now as they were during his life and some commentators finding fault with everything he did. In the following pages I have attempted to give a clear and straightforward account of the key moments in Churchill's life in order to gain some perspective on the man without being overly biased by the extremes of the debate surrounding him. This is not intended to be a full account of his life and, even if it was, it could not hope to compete with the official biography, begun by Randolph Churchill and completed by Martin Gilbert, which extends to eight volumes and over 9,000 pages. It is more of an introduction to Churchill's extraordinary life, which covers the terrible mistakes as well as the great triumphs.

But no account of Churchill could possibly be accurate without concentrating on his involvement with war and, specifically, on his leadership in the Second World War. And, whatever opinions people hold about Churchill, it is hard to argue (although some critics have tried) that he emerges from the Second World War with anything other than huge credit. As dispassionate as this account of his life attempts to be, in the end it is difficult to regard him as anything other than a remarkable man.

On a personal note I would like to acknowledge the assistance I have received from the publishers of this book, particularly Ion Mills, Claire Watts and Nick Rennison. I would also like to thank John Waters, without whom I would not be doing this, and Glenn Mitchell, who has forgotten more about Churchill than I could ever know.

His Early Life

An Early Arrival

Winston Leonard Spencer Churchill was born early in the morning of 30 November 1874 in Blenheim Palace, the huge country house near Woodstock in Oxfordshire belonging to the Dukes of Marlborough. As he would throughout his life, he gave the impression of being in a hurry even as a newborn baby, arriving more than a month prematurely and only eight months after his parents, Lord and Lady Randolph Churchill, were married. Needless to say, the short interval between the marriage and the birth has led to much speculation that he was conceived before the wedding, but, while this is entirely possible, it is equally likely that he was simply born prematurely.

At the time of his birth, the Churchills were staying at Blenheim as a temporary measure while a house in London his parents had rented was being made ready. They had made few preparations for the arrival of a baby at that particular moment, as they surely would have done had they not been taken by surprise by the early arrival. A local Woodstock doctor attended the birth rather than their London obstetrician, who could not get to the house in time, and Lord Randolph would later write to his mother-in-law that the birth had taken place a few days after Lady Randolph had fallen while out walking.

Whatever the truth of the matter, neither the young

Churchill nor his mother appears to have suffered any seriously adverse effects from his abrupt entry into the world. He was named Winston after one of his more illustrious ancestors, Sir Winston Churchill (1620–1688), the man who began the family's rise to prominence, and Leonard after Lady Randolph's father Leonard Jerome, a wealthy New York businessman and financial speculator with a rather colourful past. His surname of Spencer Churchill is usually not hyphenated and, following on from his father, he would almost always drop Spencer from his name and refer to himself simply as Churchill.

The Churchills

They may have been born more than two centuries apart, but the two Winston Churchills had more in common than their names. At different stages in their lives, both were soldiers, writers and politicians. The first Sir Winston came from a prominent but by no means aristocratic West Country family who were farmers and landowners in Devon and Dorset. Winston was the maiden name of the first Sir Winston's mother Sarah, the daughter of Sir Henry Winston of Gloucestershire, and the continuance of her family name in the Christian name of her son could well have been a way of acknowledging that her family had a higher social standing than did her husband's.

Sir Winston served as a Cavalier captain in the English Civil War (1642 to 1651) and his allegiance to the Royalist side cost him dearly after victory for the Parliamentarians, who levied a huge fine on him which would leave him in relative poverty for many years. The restoration of the monarchy in 1660 led to an improvement in his fortunes and he became a Member of Parliament in the following year. He held a number of positions in the Government, including Commissioner for Irish Land Claims, and was given some recompense for the money he had lost to the Parliamentarians. But the newly restored King Charles II was himself financially stretched and, rather than make full restitution, he appointed two of Churchill's children to positions in the royal household. Sir Winston's eldest daughter Arabella Churchill (1648–1730) became Maid of Honour to the Duchess of York, the wife of James, Duke of York, who would succeed Charles II on the throne in 1685 as King James II.

John Churchill (1650–1722) followed his sister Arabella into service in the same household, becoming page to the Duke of York and, from there, developing a career in the military. He advanced quickly, in part because of his own talent and courage, but also because of the patronage of the future king. During the Glorious Revolution of 1688, Churchill abandoned his patron to support William and Mary, who became joint monarchs. One of their first actions on their coronation was to honour Churchill with the title of the Earl of Marlborough, apparently confirming the widely held opinion that he had deserted James principally for his own advancement.

Churchill is now remembered chiefly as a British commander in the forces of the Grand Alliance during the War of the Spanish Succession and, in particular, for the victory he won at the Battle of Blenheim in 1704. Queen Anne, who succeeded to the throne in 1702 and was a close confidant of Churchill's wife Sarah, elevated him to a dukedom as a reward for the victory, which was a major turning point in the war. She also gave him the estate in Woodstock along with the money to build the spectacular house, designed by Sir John Vanbrugh, which stands there today.

The Duke of Marlborough died in 1722 with no heir, so his titles passed to his grandson Charles Spencer, the son of his second daughter Anne and the Earl of Sunderland.[1] The subsequent Dukes of Marlborough, it is fair to say, didn't live up to the example set by the first Duke, often being better known for their dissolute lifestyles and attempts to squander the family fortune than for any form of public service. In 1817, the fifth Duke legally changed the family name to Spencer-Churchill, perhaps in the hope that some of the former prestige of the Churchill name would rub off on him but, in truth, the family remained in the background of public life until Lord Randolph Churchill, the third son of the seventh Duke, entered politics in the late 1870s. He rose rapidly through the ranks of the Conservative Party before briefly serving as Chancellor of the Exchequer and Leader of the House of Commons.

In pursuing his own political career, there can be little doubt that Winston Churchill saw himself as following in the footsteps of his father. In his early years in the House of Commons, the subjects of his own campaigns and speeches followed those of Lord Randolph and, in this way, he gives the impression of attempting to vindicate his father's ultimately unsuccessful career. The extent to which he was influenced by what he knew of Marlborough is harder to gauge but it is not difficult to trace his fascination with military affairs to his ancestor, not least because of the example the Duke provided of the opportunities for personal advancement that war offered. The lives of the two Churchills were separated by more than a hundred and fifty years but, in many ways, Winston Churchill's own life had more in common with that of an eighteenth-century gentleman than it did with those of his political peers.

Young Winston

Towards the end of 1876, Lord Randolph moved to Ireland with his wife and two-year-old son to become secretary to his father, the Duke of Marlborough, who had been appointed Lord Lieutenant of Ireland by Benjamin Disraeli, the Prime Minister of the Conservative Government. Although it appeared to be a prominent position, equivalent to that of viceroy, the role of Lord Lieutenant was more that of a figure-head than one carrying any real power and there was a hint of banishment from Westminster about Marlborough's appointment. His eldest son, the Marquis of Blandford, who would succeed him as Duke, had been named in a number of divorce proceedings, one of which had almost led to the involvement of the Prince of Wales, the future King Edward VII. This would have been deeply embarrassing to the royal family and, by extension, to the British Government. By sending Marlborough to Ireland, the Government could have been punishing the Churchill family, removing the source of the embarrassment from the centre of public life.

Lord and Lady Randolph moved into a house known as the Little Lodge in Phoenix Park, a large area of open parkland in the north of Dublin. It was a short walk from the Viceregal Lodge and features in many of Winston Churchill's earliest memories, as he related in *My Early Life*, the memoirs he wrote in 1930. He also recalled the distant relationship he had with his parents, who were frequently away on official business or private engagements. The upbringing of their son was mostly left in the hands of a nanny, Mrs Elizabeth Everest, a frequent enough arrangement among the aristocracy at the time, and the young Winston who called her 'Woom' or sometimes 'Woomany', formed a close attachment to her which would endure until her death in 1895.

In *My Early Life* Churchill wrote that he could only remember having two or three significant conversations with his father and, although he certainly saw more of his mother, he very obviously felt her frequent absences deeply. He went on to write that his mother always attracted attention in public because of her radiant beauty, going on to say:

> My mother made the same brilliant impression upon my child's eye. She shone for me like an Evening Star. I loved her dearly – but at a distance.

Churchill was a boisterous and unruly child, often getting into trouble and exhibiting what we might now describe as attention-seeking behaviour. Lord and Lady Churchill employed a governess towards the end of their time in Ireland, perhaps in an attempt to bring some discipline into his life, and she introduced him to lessons which, he would recall, felt like an interruption from the much more important business of playing with his toys.

On 4 February 1880, Lady Randolph gave birth to her second son, who was named John Strange Spencer Churchill and became known as Jack. Persistent rumours have suggested that Lord Randolph was not Jack's father and, while there is no direct evidence to support this, Lady Randolph is known to have had a number of affairs at this time. Colonel John Strange Jocelyn, the fifth Earl of Roden, was thirty years older than

Lady Randolph, but is nevertheless thought to have been one of her lovers and, if he was Jack's natural father, it might perhaps account for his unusual middle name.

The Duke of Marlborough's tenure as Lord Lieutenant came to an end in 1880. The Churchills returned to England to live in London, where Lord Randolph embarked on a political career. He had been the Conservative MP for Woodstock since 1874 but, until his return from Ireland, had given few indications of any intention to take politics seriously. Suddenly he began to make speeches in the House of Commons, often attacking the leaders of his own party more vindictively than the opposition. Despite making numerous enemies, Lord Randolph rapidly rose through the ranks of the Conservative Party, becoming part of a group of young MPs sometimes known as the Fourth Party and considered more progressive than the old guard who sat on the front benches.

By this time Lord and Lady Churchill were leading almost entirely separate lives, with each of them conducting a string of affairs, mostly with the full knowledge of the other. Such behaviour was generally tolerated amongst the aristocracy at that time, as long as the affairs were conducted discreetly, but the Churchills' complicated personal lives, together with Lord Randolph's burgeoning political career, meant that they continued to see very little of their two sons. In 1881, at the age of seven, Winston was sent away to school, going to a preparatory school in Ascot. Even by the standards of the day, the headmaster was a strict disciplinarian, frequently flogging the boys under his care with the birch for the least indiscretion. Churchill described himself at this time as being 'troublesome', so it is not hard to imagine that he endured a number of these beatings himself. After attending this school for two years he became ill. His parents removed him and sent him to another school in Brighton which was much more relaxed, although not as academically rigorous, where the now nine-year-old Winston was much happier.

After three years in Brighton, Churchill moved on to Harrow School, one of the foremost public schools in Britain. He is often portrayed as doing very poorly at Harrow and, in his memoirs, he emphasises his failings, mostly for comic effect. While there is an element of truth in this version, in reality the story is a little more complicated. In some subjects he certainly didn't excel, particularly Classics and Maths, but in the subjects that he found interesting, such as English and History, he appears to have been an able student, attracting the attention of the headmaster and some of his teachers and exhibiting an impressive capacity to memorise and recite texts.

After a little over a year at Harrow, Churchill transferred to the Army Class, a separate stream in the school where boys of different ages were taught a specific curriculum aimed at preparing them for entry into the Royal Military Academy at Sandhurst. The future direction of Churchill's life was set out for him at the age of thirteen, the result of his father seeing his son's extensive collection of toy soldiers. At the time Churchill took this as a sign that his mostly absent father was taking an interest in him, although he would later discover that Lord Randolph thought the army would be a suitable career for his son because he was not bright enough to qualify for the Bar.[2]

A Young Man in a Hurry

Soldier and Writer

It took Churchill three attempts and a period of intensive cramming in Maths to pass the entrance exam for Sandhurst and then, much to the annoyance of his father, he only did well enough to be offered a cavalry cadetship. The marks required to be accepted into the cavalry were lower than those for the infantry for the simple reason that more boys applied for the infantry because, since cavalry cadets had to buy and keep their own horses, it was less expensive. Lord Randolph, who would be footing the bill, might not have been happy but Winston was delighted with the cavalry, not least because he loved horse riding. While at Sandhurst, he would develop into an accomplished polo player, incurring an even greater expense for his father by hiring a string of polo ponies.

Sandhurst was much more to Churchill's liking than Harrow. The practical nature of the course suited him down to the ground and, as he could see the purpose of what he was being taught, he began to do well. His energy and enthusiasm had previously been undirected, perhaps accounting for his unruly behaviour, but at Sandhurst he found a vocation and, for the most part, the discipline required to go with it. At the same time his father began to pay more attention to him, perhaps recognising this new-found sense of maturity in his son.

However, as Winston progressed through the course at Sandhurst, it was becoming increasingly apparent to him that his father was unwell.

In December 1894, Churchill passed out of Sandhurst, finishing a very creditable eighth out of a class of 150, demonstrating how capable he could be when he put his mind to the task at hand. On leaving Sandhurst he was commissioned as a subaltern, the lowest officer rank, in the 4th Queen's Own Hussars, a cavalry regiment which had recently returned to England from Ireland and was commanded by Colonel Brabazon, on old friend of the Churchill family from their Dublin days. At almost the same time, on 24 January 1895, Lord Randolph died, having being diagnosed as suffering from tertiary syphilis. Churchill was not aware of the nature of his father's illness (some doubt has been cast on the diagnosis since) and he must surely have felt deeply the loss of his father at just the moment when the two of them were finally beginning to develop a relationship. But he also felt a certain sense of liberation, as if he now no longer had to seek approval for his actions. For the first time in his life Churchill was responsible for himself, allowing him to make his own decisions and to follow his own path.

A further consequence of his father's death was that the twenty-year-old Churchill developed a conviction that the Churchills died young. His father was only 45 when he died and his uncle, the eighth Duke of Marlborough, had died a few years previously at the age of 48. Churchill became convinced that, if he was going to make his mark on the world, he only had a limited span of time available. In the event he lived until he was ninety, despite the alcohol and cigars, and his conviction may simply have been his own method of instilling a sense of purpose in himself so that he directed his energy towards achieving his own place in history.

Churchill's relationship with his mother began to change at this time. At Harrow he had written to her often, asking her to visit him. Her replies were infrequent and her visits even more so but, after Lord Randolph's death, they became much closer, developing a relationship which Churchill would describe as being more like that of a brother and sister than mother and son. Lady Randolph, as she continued to be called even after remarrying, was 40 when her husband died and continued to be a prominent presence in society. She would make use of her extensive network of contacts and acquaintances within the British establishment to further Winston's interests, becoming a collaborator in his attempts to realise his various ambitions and she also supplemented his salary. A cavalry officer received £300 a year, which was not enough to support even those who lived relatively modestly, and Lady Randolph contributed an additional £400 to her son, giving him a total annual budget equivalent to about £40,000 today. Even so, Churchill frequently wrote to her complaining that he was short of money. She wrote back to tell him she could not provide any more money, on one occasion writing from the best hotel in Monte Carlo to inform him of her own dire financial situation.

In the spring and summer of 1895 Churchill was based at the military barracks in Aldershot where he was engaged in a constant programme of drilling and cavalry manoeuvres. He also played polo, a sport at which he excelled, going on to represent the regiment in tournaments and continuing to play into his fifties. In the autumn he was due two and a half months leave and he decided to use this time constructively by gaining first hand experience of a war zone. Even at this early age, he had already become aware that periods of inactivity tended to bring on the depression which, later in life, he would describe as his Black Dog.

While most of his fellow officers were making use of their leave to visit their families, Churchill, together with his regimental colleague Reginald Barnes, decided to go to Cuba to observe the Spanish campaign there against an insurrection aimed at gaining independence. The British Ambassador to Spain had been a political ally of Lord Randolph and secured the relevant permission for Churchill and Barnes to observe the Spanish operations against the Cuban guerrillas, together with introductions to the Spanish military commander. Before leaving, Churchill was commissioned by the *Daily Graphic*, an illustrated London newspaper, to report on the war, giving him his first step in a lifelong writing career and helping to pay for the expedition. He was also briefed by the director of Military Intelligence on the situation in Cuba and asked to report back on what he saw, particularly in terms of the performance of the Spanish Army and their equipment. This can be seen as the beginning of his fascination with intelligence gathering and espionage, the use of which would become prominent features of his leadership during the Second World War.

Churchill and Barnes left England by ship from Liverpool, stopping first in New York where they were met by Bourke Cockran (1854–1923), a charismatic Irish-American Congressman who was an old flame of Lady Randolph from her youth in Brooklyn. He introduced them to New York society and deeply impressed the young Churchill with his wide-ranging intellect and powerful style of oratory. On arrival in Cuba, Churchill and Barnes were received as if they were an official delegation from the British Army. After a short stay in

Havana they travelled into the interior of the island, where the fighting was at its most intense and, during their two-week stay, came under fire themselves on a number of occasions, including on Churchill's 21st birthday, much to his apparent delight.

The Cuban episode only lasted for two months in total and is often hardly mentioned in accounts of Churchill's life. But it was a vital and formative experience for him in many ways, setting the pattern for his career in the army and giving him his first experiences of war. And, although Churchill could never be accused of lacking in self-confidence, travelling to a relatively remote part of the world under his own impetus and then finding that the impressions he recorded of the fighting were well-received in Britain must surely have encouraged him to trust his own judgement and continue on an independent path.

Empire

On returning to England, Churchill rejoined his regiment, which was posted to India in the following spring. As was customary in the British Army, officers who were going overseas for what could be many years were given six months leave before they left. Churchill decided to spend the time in London in what he would later describe as the only period of idleness he experienced in his life, although he would throw himself into the social scene with characteristic vigour, taking the opportunity to built up his own network of useful contacts which he could make use of at a future date. On one occasion he was invited to a dinner party by his Aunt Lilian, the widow of the eighth Duke of Marlborough, at which the Prince of

Wales was also due to attend. Unfortunately Churchill managed to make a very poor impression by turning up twenty minutes late and the Prince, who was not used to being kept waiting for dinner, was not amused. The situation was made worse for Churchill by the presence of Colonel Brabazon, his commanding officer. The Prince, who already knew Churchill and is rumoured to have had an affair with Lady Randolph, regained his good humour at the dinner table and Churchill attempted to learn a lesson from it, although punctuality would never be one of his strong points.

In *My Early Life* Churchill describes this period with a good deal of nostalgia, saying:

> In those days English Society still existed in its old form. It was a brilliant and powerful thing, with standards of conduct and methods of enforcing them now altogether forgotten. In a very large degree every one knew every one else and who they were. The few hundred great families who had governed England for so many generations and had seen her rise to the greatness of her glory, were inter-related to an enormous extent by marriage. Everywhere one met friends and kinsfolk.

To an extent this is Churchill as an older man looking back at his lost youth, but it also provides a reminder of Churchill's aristocratic background. He was a member of this ruling class who, as he says, had governed for generations and he goes on to be almost scornful of the more democratic age he lived through. He would also cling on to many of the opinions he formed as a young man concerning the superiority of the English gentleman over just about everybody else and the benefits that the British had brought to the countries of the Empire.

At the time Churchill certainly had no qualms about exploiting his privileged position for all it was worth, pulling as many strings as he could to further his own advantage. At another occasion at his aunt's house he made the acquaintance of Major-General Sir Bindon Blood who, as well as being equipped with a fine Victorian name, had recently returned from the North West Frontier, the border between Afghanistan and what is now Pakistan. Blood promised to allow Churchill to join him should any more trouble erupt and he be recalled to the frontier.

The 4th Hussars were being sent to Bangalore to provide what would be little more than a token British military presence in an entirely peaceful region of India. This prospect was not at all to Churchill's liking and he made vigorous efforts to avoid going, on one occasion being rebuffed by Sir Herbert (later Lord) Kitchener in his efforts to join the British expeditionary force which was then slowly progressing up the Nile to engage the Khalifa's rebel army in Sudan. The Khalifa was the successor to the Mahdi, whose revolt in the early 1880s had resulted in the death of General Gordon in Khartoum, and Kitchener was leading a campaign to recapture the territory lost to the revolt and to avenge the death of Gordon.

With no chance of seeing action, Churchill left England with his regiment for Bangalore, spending nine months there living the comfortable life of a colonial officer. He rented a bungalow with two other officers, took on a number of servants and decided to use his time, when he was not drilling at the barracks or playing polo, to put himself through an intensive programme of self-education by reading for four or five hours every afternoon. He read Gibbon's *Decline and Fall of the Roman Empire* and the historical works of Thomas Macaulay, paying particular attention to the use of language by these writers, together with anything he could find on politics and philosophy.

The following summer he managed to arrange leave to go to Cyprus to report on the Greco-Turkish War but, by the time the ship he was travelling on reached Italy, the war was over. He carried on to London and made himself known to the Conservative Central Office, suggesting himself as a future parliamentary candidate and accepting an invitation to make his first political speech at a rally in Bath. Churchill had a slight speech impediment and, knowing the importance of oratory in politics, worked hard to minimise the effect this would have on his public speaking. In the event the speech was a success, at least according to Churchill, and in later life he would become one of the best known orators of his time. The slight pauses in the flow of his words, more than likely his method of dealing with his impediment, actually added to the rhetorical force of his speech.

While in England Churchill read about the forthcoming military campaign being planned against the Pathan tribes in the Chitral region of the North West Frontier. Sir Bindon Blood was assembling what became known as the Malakand Field Force to advance through the Malakand Pass near the Afghan border with the intention of punishing the Pathans for their raids against the British garrisons in the region. Churchill sent a telegram to Blood reminding him of his promise and, without waiting for a reply, set out for India immediately. En route he found out that Blood didn't have any vacant positions for an officer, but Sir Bindon suggested to Churchill that he come to the front anyway as a correspondent. After securing permission from his commanding officer in Bangalore,

Churchill set out for the North West Frontier, a journey of more than 2,000 miles.

Churchill joined the Malakand Field Force in September 1896, having secured commissions to write daily reports on the campaign for the *Daily Telegraph* and the *Allahabad Pioneer*. He joined one of the three brigades of the field force and rode out with a Sikh regiment which, as was customary, was commanded by British officers. Churchill entered a valley with a detachment of Sikhs and came under fire almost immediately. Bullets flew around him which injured the two officers standing next to him. In letters he wrote later he described the action as 'hot', with the Pathans at one stage being less than forty yards away. He also recounted how he attempted to rescue a wounded officer but was driven back by the Pathans and then could do nothing but watch as they hacked the man to death with swords.

The detachment retreated from the valley and Churchill was ordered to accompany the wounded back to the main brigade. He asked to have the order in writing, even though they were under intense fire at the time, so that he could prove he was not leaving voluntarily. This insistence on committing everything to paper would become a feature of Churchill's life throughout his career in the army and as a politician, allowing him to keep a record of everything he did which he could consult when he came to write about the events at a later date.

Over the following few weeks Churchill was involved in a number of further actions and skirmishes with the Pathans, later saying that he had come under fire fifteen times. As a result of his conspicuous bravery, which was on occasion quite reckless, he was mentioned in despatches and he wrote to his mother to say that he was taking risks, but he was 'playing for high-stakes' in order to make a name for himself.

The Malakand Field Force withdrew from the pass, destroying houses and crops to punish the Pathans. It had been a dirty little war in which both sides had committed atrocities, including the killing of prisoners and wounded men. On returning to his regiment in Bangalore, Churchill used his spare afternoons to write an account of the campaign based on his own experiences and those of other officers who had taken part. He finished the manuscript in January 1898 and sent it to his mother, asking her if she could get it published for him. The subsequent book, *The Story of the Malakand Field Force*, was published in March of that year and was well-received in Britain, including by the Prime Minister, Lord Salisbury, and the Prince of Wales.

Churchill continued to write after finishing *The Story of the Malakand Field Force*, working on a novel he had begun the previous year which would be published as *Savrola* in 1900. It was a romantic story of a rebellion against the dictatorial leader of a fictitious southern European country, led by the title character who was clearly based on Churchill himself. It earned Churchill £700, almost as much as his yearly income at the time, but he doesn't appear to have been very proud of the finished book, suggesting to his friends that they would be better off by not reading what would become his only published work of fiction.

While writing *Savrola*, and when he was not playing polo, Churchill was doing everything he could to join Kitchener's army in Sudan, where the campaign against the Khalifa was gradually coming to a climax. In June of 1898 he returned to London on yet another leave to further his plans, having encountered resistance from Kitchener, who regarded

Churchill as a glory hunter and self-publicist. As Sirdar, or Commander-in-Chief, of the Egyptian Army, Kitchener could control the appointment of officers and was not going to take on Churchill, even after Churchill had persuaded Lord Salisbury to take his side. In the end Churchill secured an attachment to the 21st Lancers, a regiment that was already in Egypt but remained a part of the British Army, with officers appointed directly from the War Office in London. Needless to say, Kitchener was not overly impressed when he found out that Churchill had circumvented his wishes in this way, but he did nothing further to stop him coming to the Sudan.

Churchill set out immediately for Cairo, having already been commissioned by the *Morning Post* to write articles at £15 a column. He joined up with the Lancers in the middle of August and travelled up the Nile, reaching Kitchener's army near Khartoum only just in time for the Battle of Omdurman, which began on 2 September. Early in the morning of that day, Churchill led a small party of Lancers on a scouting mission to the top of a low hill separating the 50,000-strong Dervish army from Kitchener's forces, which had about half that strength. Churchill observed the Dervish army advancing, sending a message back to Kitchener and then waiting until the forward ranks of the Dervishes were within 400 yards and rifle bullets were going over his head before retiring.

The Dervishes were armed with rifles and spears and proved no match for the artillery, volley fire and Maxim guns of the British. The main part of the battle lasted about two hours before the Dervishes were forced to withdraw, leaving thousands of casualties on the battlefield. The 21st Lancers, including Churchill, had remained in camp and he did not actually witness this phase of the battle but, with the Dervishes retreating, the cavalry unit was ordered forward to clear a path through the retreating army towards Omdurman and the Khalifa's camp. The 300-strong Lancers attacked what they thought was a party of about 150 Dervish infantry which stood between them and the main body of the Dervish forces and appeared to be armed only with spears. As they got closer the Dervishes began to open up with rifle-fire but, rather than retire, the Lancers wheeled round into a line facing them and advanced into a full charge. There turned out to be more than 2,000 Dervishes immediately behind the others, hidden from view in a dry watercourse, but the Lancers continued into the middle of these massed ranks. Churchill went down into the bed of the watercourse where he was surrounded by men. He pushed his way through them and up the other side, recounting in *My Early Life*:

> Once again I was on hard, crisp desert, my horse at a trot. I had the impression of scattered dervishes running to and fro in all directions. Straight before me a man threw himself on the ground... I saw the gleam of his curved sword as he drew it back for a ham-stringing cut. I had room and time enough to turn my pony out of his reach, and leaning over on the offside I fired two shots into him at about three yards. As I straightened myself into the saddle, I saw before me another figure with uplifted sword. I raised my pistol and fired. So close were we that the pistol itself actually struck him. Man and sword disappeared below and behind me.

Churchill rejoined his men, finding himself completely unscathed. The Lancers had lost five officers and sixty-five men, almost a quarter of their total strength, and rather than continue after the retreating Dervish soldiers and engage them with a second charge, as Churchill had initially wanted to do, they used their rifles. The charge was one of the last occasions when this tactic was used on such a scale by the British Army and resulted in the award of three Victoria Crosses. It was not a decisive moment in the battle but it succeeded in pushing the Dervish army back, who were then routed by British infantry later in the day.

With the cavalry no longer needed in Sudan, Churchill returned to London, where he made a number of further speeches at Tory Party rallies. By November he was back in India, primarily to compete in the prestigious Inter-Regimental Polo Tournament, which was held in February 1899. The 4th Hussars won the tournament for the first and only time in their history. Churchill played in every game, despite being hampered by an injured shoulder, which he had wrenched when first arriving in India and which would continue to give him problems for many years. He was also writing up his account of the campaign in Sudan, basing his book on his newspaper reports. Published in two volumes in 1899, as *The River War*, it contained a number of criticisms of Kitchener, particularly for allowing his army to kill wounded Dervish soldiers and for the desecration of the Mahdi's tomb in Khartoum in the aftermath of the battle.

Shortly after the polo tournament Churchill resigned his commission and returned to England to prepare for the beginning of his political career. His first opportunity came at a by-election in Oldham in July, where he stood as one of the two Conservative candidates for the ward. Despite an enthusiastic campaign, he was ultimately unsuccessful, polling about a thousand fewer votes than the successful Liberal candidates. In the circumstances, with the incumbent Conservative

Government pushing through some unpopular policies at the time, it was a creditable performance, but the loss left Churchill without a job. Needless to say, it didn't take him long to move on to the next stage of his grand plan.

The Boer War

During the summer and autumn of 1899 it was becoming increasingly apparent that the British Empire was heading for a confrontation with the independent Boer republics of Transvaal and the Orange Free State and, although no longer in the army, Churchill was determined to get to the scene of the action. Before war was formally declared on 11 October, he had arranged a lucrative contract with the *Morning Post*, which offered to pay him £250 a month plus expenses for a minimum period of four months, making him the highest paid corre-spondent covering the war.

Churchill left for the Cape a few days after war was declared, travelling on the same ship as Sir Redvers Buller, the commander-in-chief of the British forces. On arrival he set out for Natal, where the Boer army had mounted a pre-emptive strike against Ladysmith which would develop into a protracted siege. The railway line into the town had been cut, preventing Churchill reaching the city, and he joined the British forces further down the line. On 15 November he accompanied Captain Aylmer Haldane, whom he had known on the North West Frontier, and a detachment of about 150 British soldiers on a reconnaissance mission by armoured train towards Ladysmith. The train came under sustained attack by Boer artillery and rifle-fire and, when attempting to withdraw at speed, the three carriages at the rear of the train became derailed, blocking the track. While Haldane commanded the British response to the attack, Churchill took control of the attempts being made to clear the track, using the engine, which had been in the middle of the six carriages originally making up the train, to push the derailed carriages out of the way. He then helped to load wounded soldiers onto the engine, at considerable personal risk, and accompanied it as it headed out of the danger area. On the way back to help Haldane, Churchill encountered two Boer soldiers and, in an effort to escape from them, ran into another Boer who was mounted on a horse and pointing his rifle at him. He realised that he had taken his pistol off while loading the wounded onto the engine and, finding himself unarmed, was forced to surrender.

The prisoners from the train were taken to Pretoria where they were held in a school which had been converted into a prison camp. Over the next three weeks Churchill wrote a number of letters to the Boer authorities explaining that he was a journalist and, as a non-combatant who was not armed at the time of his capture, should be released. The Boers were well aware of his role in the events of that day, because it had been widely reported in the newspapers in Britain, and they refused. Churchill wrote again to offer his parole, saying that he would not take up arms against the Boers and would return to England if they let him go.

By the second week of December, since he had not heard back from the Boer authorities, Churchill decided to attempt an escape, persuading Haldane and their fellow prisoner Sergeant-Major Brokie to include him in a plan they had been working on to climb over the wall of the prison latrine at night. During the evening of 12 December, Churchill entered the latrine on his own, expecting Haldane and Brokie to follow him, and, recognising an opportunity to get over the wall without the prison guards seeing him, he climbed out and waited for the other two to follow him. After more than an hour Churchill could wait no longer and set off on his own even though he had very little food with him and could not speak Dutch. The only other option was to climb back into the prison, but this did not stop later allegations that Churchill's lone escape had compromised the chances of his two colleagues. It has also been alleged that Churchill was breaking parole by escaping, even though at the time of the escape it had not been formally accepted.

After escaping Churchill found himself alone in Pretoria, in the middle of enemy territory. Acting as nonchalantly as he could, he walked through the city and, as he was wearing civilian clothes, was ignored by everybody he passed. His plan was to head for Lourenço Marques, a port on the coast of Portuguese East Africa, now Maputo in Mozambique, which was 300 miles away but linked to Pretoria by a railway line. When he was outside the city, and in the dark, he managed to climb aboard a goods train, without being certain in which direction it was heading, and hid himself under some empty coal sacks.

In the morning Churchill left the train and sheltered in a tree where, he would later write, he was kept company by a large vulture. With no food and little idea where he was, he decided to approach a house and ask for help. By this time a huge search operation had been mounted by the Boer authorities who issued a remarkably accurate description of him:

Englishman 25 years old, about 5ft 8 inches tall [he was actually 5ft 6 1/2"], average build, walks with a slight stoop, pale appearance, red brown hair, almost invisible small moustache, speaks through the nose, cannot pronounce the letter "s", cannot speak Dutch, has last been seen in a brown suit of clothes.

He approached a house next to a coal mine and knocked on the door. Much to his good fortune, it was answered by John Howard, a British-born mine manager who had remained in the Transvaal after the war had started, together with a few British miners, to ensure that the mine workings were maintained. Howard hid Churchill in the mine shaft for a few days and then in the back room of the office building while he arranged a method of escape. He was then concealed in a space that had been left for him in the middle of a consignment of bales of wool which had been loaded on a goods train for transport to Lourenço Marques. Three days later he emerged from the bales in Lourenço Marques and went immediately to the British Consulate.

The war had not been going well for Britain at this time. Churchill's escape coincided with what became known as Black Week, when British forces were defeated three times in a matter of days, incurring a considerable number of casualties. As a result, his exploits were reported extensively in the British newspapers, serving as a distraction for what would otherwise have been a constant flow of bad news. When reports reached Britain that his escape had been successful, he became something of a national hero, fulfilling his aim of getting his name known across the country.

Rather than return to Britain immediately, Churchill accepted a commission into the South African Light Horse, an irregular cavalry regiment which appealed to him because it allowed him the freedom to continue his reporting for the

Morning Post and because he liked the wide-brimmed hat with a large feather in its band which was part of the uniform. He also secured a commission for his younger brother Jack to join him in the regiment, although this arrangement didn't last very long. Shortly after arriving in South Africa and while lying on the ground next to Winston, Jack was wounded in the calf, reportedly prompting Churchill, who had not received so much as a scratch in any of the fighting he had taken part in, to say, 'Jack, you silly ass. You've only been here five minutes and you've got yourself shot'.

In typical fashion, Churchill managed to be present at many of the main encounters between the two sides during the six months he remained in the country, fighting at the disastrous Battle of Spion Kop and the Relief of Ladysmith. He also accompanied the force led by Sir Ian Hamilton as it advanced northwards from Bloemfontein into the heartland of enemy territory and was amongst the first to enter both Johannesburg and Pretoria. After one encounter Hamilton wrote of Churchill's conspicuous gallantry in advancing to a highly exposed position so that he could send signals back to the British forces of the position of the Boer army. Such words from a commanding officer would normally lead to the award of a medal for bravery but no recommendation was made for Churchill. This may have been the result of the criticisms he had persistently made of senior military figures in his reports and books, together with the widely-held perception in military circles that he was only in the army in the first place to further his own ambitions.

While he was still in South Africa, Churchill compiled his newspaper reports into two books, *London to Ladysmith via Pretoria* and *Ian Hamilton's March*, both of which were published

in 1900. By June of that year, the war was dominated by guerrilla tactics and Churchill, aware that a general election would
shortly be called in Britain, resigned his commission for the
second time and travelled home, arriving in Southampton
towards the end of July. From then on, he devoted himself to
pursuing a political career.

Rise and Fall

The Political Animal

The general election of 1900, which became known as the 'Khaki election' because of the influence of the war, was called in October by the Prime Minister Lord Salisbury. The timing was intentional, with the Conservative administration hoping to exploit the wave of nationalist feeling sweeping the country on the back of the successful campaigns in South Africa. Churchill stood again in the working class district of Oldham, hoping that the fame he had found during the war would be enough to reverse the result of the by-election a year previously. He embarked on another bout of rigorous campaigning, making speech after speech and often referring to his experiences in South Africa, helped on one occasion by the presence in the crowd of the wife of one of the miners who had helped him to escape.

Churchill came second in the Oldham election which, as the Oldham ward returned two MPs, meant that he had succeeded in entering Westminster, at the age of only 26. At that time MPs were unpaid (they first received a salary in 1911), so before taking up his seat, Churchill went on an extensive speaking tour of Britain, lecturing on his war experiences with the aid of a magic lantern to audiences of thousands in 29 cities and earning a percentage of the takings, which regularly came to more than £200 a night. He followed this up with a tour to North America where, in New York, his lecture was introduced by Mark Twain who commented on Churchill's American heritage and attempted to smooth over the pro-Boer sympathies that he and many of the people in the audience held. Churchill was heckled on a few occasions during his lectures in America, by Irish Americans with nationalist leanings as well as by those who were pro-Boer, but he received an easier ride in Canada where he was when, on 22 January 1901, he learned of the death of Queen Victoria.

Churchill returned to Britain in February to take up his seat in the House of Commons. Over the previous two years he had earned about £10,000 from writing and speaking which, even taking his profligate lifestyle into account, was enough for him to live on for at least the next five years. In his maiden speech to the House he touched on a number of themes which would preoccupy him in the future. He criticised the Government's handling of the Boer War and he also referred to the political career of his father. Over the coming months he made a number of further speeches and took part in several debates, being openly critical of his own party's leadership. He became associated with a group of young and mostly aristocratic Tory MPs known as the Hughligans, named after Sir Hugh Cecil, one of the leading members of the group and the son of Lord Salisbury. They considered the party leadership to be old-fashioned and out of touch and agitated for change.

In the official biography of his life, his son Randolph wrote of the hectic schedule Churchill set for himself at this time, leading an incredibly active social life as well as being busy in Parliament:

Altogether in the eleven months of 1901 he made nine speeches in the House, some thirty speeches in the country and lectured in twenty towns. He gave up twelve afternoons to polo, fourteen days to hunting and two days to shooting, and spent eighteen days on holiday abroad.

As his appointments diary from 1901 shows, he also had frequent lunch and dinner engagements with various members of his family and with friends and colleagues. He saw a great deal of his cousin Sunny, the eighth Duke of Marlborough, who had been with him in South Africa and had lent Churchill the use of his London apartment. His life in London, much as it had been in the army, was a blur of activity as he continued to explore every opportunity to advance himself.

Over the next few years Churchill took up the cause of free trade, as his father had done twenty years before. The government was considering introducing tariffs on goods imported into Britain from outside the Empire, a policy opposed by the Liberals as a form of protectionism which would prove economically damaging in the long term. Churchill found his own views were becoming increasingly aligned with those of the Liberals. As long ago as 1897 he had written to his mother from India to say that, 'I am a Liberal in all but name'. Had it not been for his aristocratic and military background, it appears likely he would have joined them rather than the Conservatives in the first place. As early as 1902 he was advocating the establishment of a new political party to occupy the middle ground, one which, in his own words, would be 'free at once from the sordid selfishness and callousness of Toryism on the one hand, and the blind appetites of the radical masses on the other'.

At the same time Churchill was becoming increasingly

concerned with the issues surrounding social reform, writing on one occasion, ' I see little glory in an Empire which can rule the waves and is unable to flush its sewers'. Towards the end of 1903, when Arthur Balfour, who had replaced Salisbury as Prime Minister, proposed introducing tariffs on imports, Churchill's continued membership of the Conservative Party appeared to have become almost untenable. He described the protectionist policies as ones which would lead to 'dear food for the million, cheap labour for the millionaire'. The only remaining obstacle to him joining the Liberals was their support for Irish Home Rule, to which he, like his father before him, was vehemently opposed.

The Liberal association in the North-West Manchester ward offered to allow him to stand as an independent free trade candidate in the next election, a move which enabled him to leave the Conservatives and join the Liberals gradually. Even some of the leadership of the Conservative Party recognised that it was now inevitable that Churchill would change parties and, when he reached an accommodation with the Liberals over Irish Home Rule, the stage was set for him to 'cross the floor', the phrase used to describe moving from one political party to another in the House of Commons.

On 31 May 1904, the first day of Parliament after the Whitsun recess, Churchill entered the Chamber and, instead of turning left to take his seat on the Conservative benches, he turned right towards the Liberal opposition, taking a seat next to the radical Welsh MP David Lloyd George. From that moment on many Conservatives regarded him as a traitor, labelling him a 'turncoat' and a 'cad'. It was alleged that the main reasons for changing party were those of self-interest, and that he had realised that the Liberal opposition could offer him better opportunities for his personal advancement.

During such a busy and tumultuous period of his political career, it is perhaps surprising that Churchill found the time to continue writing. But he had begun a major biography of his father in 1903 and would continue to work on it intermittently over the next few years. It was published in two volumes in 1906 and attracted considerable critical attention at the time, almost all of it favourable, although it is now considered to be overly sympathetic to its subject and selective in its use of source material.

Churchill's social life also continued at its usual hectic pace, although he was shunned in some quarters by diehard Tories. That summer he attended a ball with his mother where he was introduced to the 19-year-old Clementine Hozier, the daughter of one of Lady Randolph's friends. Their first meeting was not a great success, with Churchill failing to ask his future wife to dance and leaving her with the impression that he was arrogant and aloof. There was a certain amount of truth in these first impressions and it would be fair to say that two areas in which, throughout his life, Churchill never excelled were dancing and polite conversation.

In Office

If Churchill's plan really had been to join the Liberal Party to further his own career, then it certainly worked. The Conservatives had been in disarray for some time and, in December 1905, Balfour resigned as Prime Minister, hoping that apparent divisions in the Liberal Party would prevent them from forming a Government and he could begin again with a new administration. But with the prospect of gaining power in sight, the divisions between the differing factions in the Liberal Party were overcome. Henry Campbell-Bannerman became the next Prime Minister and immediately called an election, confident of winning because of the unpopularity of the Conservatives at the time.

Churchill contested the North-West Manchester seat as a Liberal candidate and, just as the Liberal Government as a whole did, he won quite comfortably. He was offered a choice of positions in the next administration, eventually becoming Under Secretary of State for the Colonies. Because the Secretary of State, Lord Elgin, sat in the House of Lords, the Under Secretary was left to conduct the department's business in the Commons. It was a junior position but it allowed Churchill to have a higher profile in the Government than he might have had if he had been given more senior positions in other departments. Despite his very obvious good health and energy, he still held to the belief that he was destined to die young and needed to make his mark as quickly as possible, so the more exposure he could gather the better. He had made no secret of his desire to become Prime Minister himself and everything he did was taken by his many opponents as nothing more than further examples of political manoeuvring to enhance his chances of achieving this aim.

Churchill immediately brought his energy to bear on the Colonial Office, unsettling many of the career civil servants working under him, most of whom were considerably older than he was and were used to working at a much more leisurely pace. He worked on a new constitution for the Transvaal and went on a long trip to the African continent, ostensibly to go hunting, but also to see for himself the condition of Britain's African colonies[3]. The long hours he worked and the desire to see things for himself would be features of much of his political career. It often infuriated those working with him, although many recognised his brilliance and had to acknowledge that, when Churchill was involved, whatever needed to be done was done quickly.

Lloyd George had become the Chancellor of the Exchequer in Campbell-Bannerman's Government and, under his influence, Churchill adopted the policies of New Liberalism which encompassed a range of social and welfare reforms and represented a move to the left by the party. In April 1908, Herbert Asquith, who had become Prime Minister after the death of Campbell-Bannerman, appointed Churchill to the post of President of the Board of Trade, a position which gave him a seat in the Cabinet. At that time newly-appointed ministers were required to seek re-election to Parliament and, at the subsequent by-election in North-West Manchester, Churchill lost his seat. It was only to prove a temporary setback because he stood at another by-election in Dundee only a few weeks later, and was returned to Parliament.

At the same time as this was going on, Churchill was reintroduced to Clementine Hozier at a dinner party and this time made a slightly better impression. They began to see each other regularly, with Churchill proving that he could be charming and attentive when he put his mind to it. That summer he invited Clementine to spend the weekend at Blenheim Palace, where he intended to ask her to marry him. After failing to pluck up the courage for the first two days, his cousin Sunny prompted him by telling him that if he didn't ask he would miss his chance. Finally he asked Clementine to accompany him on a walk by the lake in the grounds of Blenheim and, while they were in the Temple of Diana grotto next to the lake, he proposed. She accepted and, after a short engagement, they were married on 12 September 1908 at St Margaret's Church in Westminster.

The following year Winston and Clementine took a house in Eccleston Square, a short walk from Westminster. It quickly became apparent to Clementine that she was married both to him and to his political career but, even though they were apart for long periods and certainly had occasional rows, they enjoyed a long and mostly happy marriage. As far as it is possible to tell, Churchill did not follow the pattern of his parents' marriage, remaining faithful to his wife for the next fifty-five years. Of their five children, the first was a daughter, born in 1909, whom they named Diana. She was followed by Randolph, Sarah and Marigold, who died of septicaemia at the age of two. Their final daughter was born in 1922 after an interval of some years. She was called Mary and is now the Baroness Soames.

While Churchill was in the process of settling into married life and becoming a father for the first time, he was introducing a number of important pieces of legislation into the House of Commons. One bill established a minimum wage for a large group of low paid workers, mostly women working in 'sweated' labour, the first time the principle of a legally binding minimum wage had been brought into law. He also established labour exchanges in an effort to help the unemployed find work and was working on a plan for compulsory employment insurance which would become amalgamated with Lloyd George's work on medical insurance and pass into law in 1911 as part of the National Insurance Act.

Churchill and Lloyd George formed what now appears to be an unlikely alliance during this period and were responsible for bringing in legislation which anticipated the birth of the Welfare State after the Second World War. Unlike Churchill, Lloyd George was from a relatively humble background and had achieved success through his own intelligence and hard work rather than through knowing the right people. He was ten years older than Churchill and, at least at this time, was the dominant partner in the relationship, leading some commentators to describe Churchill as under the Welsh Wizard's spell.

The so-called People's Budget in 1909 introduced measures to increase the tax burden on the wealthy to pay for welfare reforms and included a form of land tax, arguably the first legislation ever brought before parliament which was directly aimed at the redistribution of wealth. The House of Lords, which was mostly made up of wealthy landowners, vetoed the budget, voting against financial legislation passed in the House of Commons for the first time in two hundred years. Their action precipitated a constitutional crisis and a general election in January 1910, fought by the Liberals mainly on the basis of support for the measures in the budget. They emerged from the vote as the largest party in Parliament, although they did not have a majority of seats and had to join in coalition with the Irish Nationalists to form a Government.

The House of Lords finally voted in favour of the budget after the land tax had been dropped and the King had threatened to create hundreds of new Liberal peers to ensure that it would go through. Another general election was held at the end of the year, again resulting in a minority Liberal Government, but giving them the mandate to challenge the power of the House of Lords. This lead to the Parliament Act of 1911, which was supported by Churchill and limited the ability of the Lords, including his cousin Sunny, to block legislation passed in the House of Commons.

Between these two elections, Herbert Asquith had promoted Churchill to Home Secretary, where he was responsible for the internal affairs of the country, including law and order. One of his duties was to confirm death sentences passed in the law courts. It was, he would later write, an onerous task and on a number of occasions he commuted the sentence to life imprisonment. He was remarkably sympathetic towards prisoners in general, initiating prison reforms and saying that his experiences as a prisoner of war in South Africa had given him an understanding of the issues involved.

While Churchill was promoting prison reform and supporting Lloyd George's welfare plans, he adopted a tough attitude towards matters of law and order. In response to the strikes in the coal mines of the Rhondda Valley in South Wales, which began in November 1910, Churchill despatched police from London to help the local force to control the situation. Rioting broke out in the village of Tonypandy and there was a confrontation between the police and the miners. The local authorities had called out units of the army, which no doubt would have made the situation much worse, but, although these soldiers were held in reserve, Churchill refused to allow them to be used against the strikers. Despite adopting a relatively moderate approach, he was accused of allowing the power he commanded to go to his head and his reputation within the labour movement in South Wales, and the Trade Unions in general, has never recovered.

Six weeks after the Tonypandy riots Churchill provided more fuel for his critics with his handling of the Siege of Sidney Street. Police had uncovered an attempt by a group of East European immigrants, described as Latvian anarchists in some accounts, to tunnel into a jewellery shop in the East End of London. Three policemen were killed in the ensuing confrontation and three of the gang, including a mysterious figure known as Peter the Painter, barricaded themselves into a house in Sidney Street, using rifles to keep the police away. A unit of the army was called out and, the next day, Churchill was asked to authorise this, which he did. He also decided to go to the scene himself in company with Edward Marsh, his long-serving private secretary, and, while they were there, newsreel footage and photographs were taken of them, both sheltering from the firing.

In one of the newsreels later shown in cinemas it was said that a bullet had gone through Churchill's hat and, whether or not this was true, he had certainly put himself in danger by his actions. He was also accused of issuing orders on the scene, which he had no authority to do, although the evidence suggests that all he did was tell the fire brigade not to approach the building after it had caught fire because the people inside were still shooting. The Conservative opposition in Parliament saw Churchill's action as yet another example of his recklessness and questioned his suitability to be Home Secretary. Commenting on the risks taken by a photographer who had taken pictures of Churchill at the scene, Balfour remarked, 'I understand what the photographer was doing, but what was the right honourable gentleman doing?'.

An ongoing problem for Churchill during his time as Home Secretary was how to deal with the suffragette movement. After he had made some injudicious remarks, saying when discussing whether women should have the vote, 'We already have enough ignorant voters and don't want any more', suffragettes organised demonstrations at his political meetings and he was assaulted in the street several times, on one occasion being struck in the face with a dog whip. After Black Friday, when police broke up a suffragette demonstration in Manchester, injuring a number of women, he refused to hold an inquiry into their actions, but he also introduced measures to ensure that suffragettes who had been sent to prison were considered as political prisoners, held because of their views and treated better than 'common criminals'.

The summer of 1911 was notable for being one of the hottest on record and for a series of strikes across Britain, with seamen, dockers and railwaymen, amongst others, all coming out to protest at their working conditions and pay. It didn't actually coalesce into a general strike but nevertheless had a serious affect on the economy of the country and presented a major challenge to the Home Secretary. Churchill's response to the miners' strike in South Wales may well have been relatively restrained, despite what his critics have claimed, but he was in no mood to continue in this manner that summer. Perhaps in reaction to the hot weather, he implemented a series of intemperate measures. He despatched army units to various locations around the country and soldiers were stationed in Hyde Park in London. He even agreed to send a warship to Liverpool to be moored by the docks, although what it was supposed to do once it was there is far from clear.

First Lord

Churchill's heavy-handed measures in dealing with the strikes only served to inflame the situation. He was widely criticised in the House of Commons and in the press for his hot-headed response which was seen as a further example of his unpredictable behaviour. The crisis was eventually sorted out by negotiation, conducted in the main by Lloyd George rather than Churchill who had, by this time, entirely lost the trust of the trade unions. The extent to which all this contributed to his move away from the Home Office is hard to tell but Asquith appears to have wanted a safer pair of hands to deal with labour relations in the future.

In October, Churchill became First Lord of the Admiralty[4]. A certain irony attached itself to these changes because Churchill had previously vigorously opposed plans for naval expenditure, particularly those for building new ships. Going from the Home Office to the Admiralty was in no sense a promotion, hardly even a sideways move, but Churchill badgered Asquith at every opportunity, perhaps realising himself that his talents would find a more suitable outlet as First Lord than as Home Secretary. Throughout his various Government jobs he had maintained his interest in military affairs and he became increasingly aware of the rising tensions between the main European powers. This had been brought sharply into focus for him by the Agadir Crisis in July 1911, a diplomatic incident that had escalated almost to the point of war when the German government sent a gunboat to the Moroccan port of Agadir in an attempt to intimidate the French. The diplomatic row that erupted over the incident eventually calmed down but it alerted Churchill to Germany's colonial ambitions and expanding sea power.

As soon as he arrived at the Admiralty Churchill was determined to introduce plans to modernise the navy and get it into a fit state to fight the major war with Germany which he was sure would come within the next few years. To this end, he created a Naval War Staff, developed plans to convert the fleet fully from coal-fired to oil-fired engines and built up the Royal Naval Air Service into a fighting force in addition to its role in reconnaissance.

The job of First Lord of the Admiralty came with a number of perks, not least of which was the use of Admiralty House in Whitehall as an official residence. It was something of a double-edged sword as the First Lord was expected to pay the wages of the staff of twelve out of his own pocket and, even though Churchill now received a salary of £2,000 as a Cabinet Minister, he was typically short of money. The *Enchantress*, the Admiralty yacht, was also at his disposal[5] and over the next three years he would make good use of it to visit many of the naval facilities around Britain and, on two occasions, to inspect the harbours of the Mediterranean.

For much of this period Churchill's energies were primarily focused on his duties at the Admiralty. The only major exception was his continued interest in Irish Home Rule. Before the Parliament Act in 1911 any attempt to introduce bills granting Ireland any form of self-rule were blocked in the House of Lords. The restriction on the powers of the Lords after 1911 meant that Home Rule became a real possibility, not least because Asquith's minority Government relied on the votes of the Irish Nationalist MPs to survive. As Europe headed for the cataclysm of the First World War, the future of Ireland was causing a crisis in Britain. Churchill had always favoured separate arrangements for the Nationalist South and Unionist North of Ireland, but his ideas were outvoted in the Cabinet, which came down in favour of Home Rule for the whole of Ireland. The Ulster Unionists rejected any thought of being governed from Dublin and a 100,000-strong militia called the Ulster Volunteers was formed with the aim of resisting any attempts to devolve power under the proposed Home Rule Act.

Churchill fell into line with the Government's policy on Home Rule for the whole of Ireland. In February 1912 he travelled to Belfast to make a speech in the same hall where his father had incited Unionists to resist any attempts to force them into joining with the South, famously remarking 'Ulster will fight and Ulster will be right'. Security fears forced Churchill to move the meeting to a Nationalist football stadium, where he set out the Government's plans to a more sympathetic audience.

By March 1914, the police reported that the Ulster Volunteers were planning to seize arms held by the British Army and take control themselves. Churchill issued orders for a squadron of naval ships to sail to the west coast of Scotland, seventy miles from Belfast, where they would be in position to put down any trouble in the city. He countermanded the order before the ships had reached their destination but knowledge of his action, which he appears to have decided upon without consulting the Cabinet, caused many of his opponents to accuse him of planning a coup in Belfast, the 'Ulster Pogrom', with the intention of crushing the Volunteers.

Shortly after this episode, the majority of the officers of a cavalry regiment based at the Curragh Camp, the main barracks for the British Army in Ireland, resigned en masse in protest at the prospect of being ordered to fight against the Ulster Volunteers. This became known as the Curragh Mutiny although, since the officers concerned resigned before any orders were issued, they did not technically mutiny. As a result, Asquith realised he could not rely on the army to put down an Ulster rebellion if they tried to force through the Home Rule Act.

Churchill became heavily involved in attempting to find a solution to this problem, favouring an arrangement which would see Ulster opt out of Home Rule. However, greater events were about to overtake everybody. On 28 June, Archduke Franz Ferdinand, the heir to the Austro-Hungarian throne, was assassinated in Sarajevo by Gavrilo Princip, a Bosnian Serb nationalist, in an act which precipitated the chain of events that led to the First World War. A month later Austria delivered a letter to Serbia containing a list of demands the Serbians would have to meet to avoid the withdrawal of Austrian diplomats from the country. The July Ultimatum, as it became known, was read out to the British Cabinet, who were discussing, in Churchill's words, 'the muddy byways of Fermanagh and Tyrone' at the time in an effort to establish where a boundary between the north and south of Ireland could be drawn. It was immediately apparent to the Cabinet that the terms set out in the ultimatum could not possibly be accepted in their entirety by Serbia but, at least at this stage, it appeared that the crisis could be dealt with by diplomacy.

The Serbian Government accepted some of the terms of the Austro-Hungarian ultimatum but, before diplomatic efforts could settle the outstanding difficulties, a minor and probably unintentional border infraction by the Serbian army towards the end of July escalated quickly into war, with the Austro-Hungarian army invading Serbia. This prompted Russia, the historic ally of Serbia, to mobilise its army against Austro-Hungary and declare war. France immediately came out in support of Russia in accordance with its treaty obligations, as did Germany in favour of Austro-Hungary. Churchill put the Royal Navy onto a war footing in preparation for Britain's entry into the war, sending the main battle fleet to Scapa Flow in the Orkneys from where it could dominate both the North Atlantic and North Sea.

At this point Britain's participation in the war was by no means certain. An agreement known as the *Entente Cordiale* existed between Britain and France but this did not extend to military assistance. On 3 August, Germany formally declared war on France. This was followed by a declaration of war against Belgium, which had refused to allow the German army to cross its territory so that it could invade France from the north, thus avoiding the French defensive fortifications along the German border. This was a clear violation of Belgium's neutrality, which was guaranteed by treaties signed by all the major powers. At a Cabinet meeting at which Churchill was present it was agreed to send an ultimatum to Germany requiring it to stop its advance on Belgium or face war with Britain. The ultimatum expired at midnight on 4 August and, as Germany had not replied, a state of war existed between the two countries.

From the very start of the war Churchill played an extremely active role in the day-to-day operations of the navy, taking the lead in formulating strategy and even, on occasions, directly issuing orders. The fleet imposed a naval blockade on Germany which would, in the long term, prove highly effective. But such naval manoeuvres don't appear to have satisfied Churchill's apparent enthusiasm for the war, which led him to look for a role for himself on land as well as at sea. He sent three squadrons of aeroplanes from the Royal Naval Air Service to northern France, together with a fleet of armour-plated Rolls Royces for their protection, to bomb the advancing German Army in an operation which became known as the 'Dunkirk Circus'. He also had at his disposal the Royal Naval

Division, a land force of about 15,000 Royal Marines and naval reservists he had created before the war, which were, in effect, his own private army and he was keen to find a use for them.

The German Army had advanced quickly through France and Belgium at the beginning of the war, pushing the French Army and British Expeditionary Force back towards Paris. The German advance was finally stopped at the First Battle of the Marne in September, preventing them from taking Paris. The Germans withdrew to a line of trenches, establishing the Western Front that would remain almost static for the next four years. In a series of manoeuvres each side attempted to outflank the other on the western edges of the defensive lines, extending the trenches towards the coast of the English Channel in what became known as the Race to the Sea. By the beginning of October, the German Army had advanced towards Antwerp, near the north coast of Belgium, and was attacking the ring of defensive forts which protected the city. It was considered a strategically important point by the British because, if the Germans captured it, as they appeared about to do, it would open the way for them to advance on the French channel ports of Dunkirk and Calais where the British were in the process of landing their forces.

In a meeting with Kitchener, the Secretary of State for War, Churchill suggested that he go to Antwerp to assess the situation personally and to stiffen the resolve of the Belgium Army. He arrived in the city on 3 October to find the defences in disarray and the army on the brink of surrender. In talks with the Belgium Government, he convinced them to continue fighting and then took command of the defence himself, ordering the Royal Naval Division into the city. The experience of commanding forces in the field was so intoxicating that, after a few days, he sent a telegram to Asquith asking if he could resign his position at the Admiralty and be given a high-ranking command in the army in France. The proposal was greeted with derision by the Cabinet and Churchill was ordered home. On 10 October, Antwerp capitulated to the Germans and Churchill was roundly criticised for his actions, although he had at least succeeded in holding up the German advance for a week, thus giving the British Expeditionary Force more time to strengthen their positions for the forthcoming First Battle of Ypres, at which the German Army was stopped. Such considerations, however, were ignored in the aftermath of the defeat at Antwerp and Churchill was cast as a power-hungry opportunist whose military adventure had damaged the war effort.

In the autumn of 1914, the Royal Navy suffered a series of setbacks, losing five cruisers in engagements with the German Navy. On each occasion the Conservative press blamed Churchill, accusing him of being an amateur and of ignoring the opinions of his professional staff. He was, they claimed, a 'Lilliput Napoleon' who was causing havoc at the Admiralty by running it to advance his own ambitions rather than for the good of the country. After the initial reversals, the Royal Navy gained the upper hand in the sea war, although the German U-boats remained a menace, but, in the minds of many people, Churchill's name was now irrevocably linked to military and naval defeats.

In October, the First Sea Lord, Prince Louis of Battenberg, was forced to resign because of his German roots. He was replaced by Lord 'Jacky' Fisher, a long-time friend and correspondent of Churchill who was almost 74 at the time of the appointment but had been considered the foremost admiral of his day. At first sight it appeared to be an ideal combination, with two such able men working together at the head of the navy, but, as subsequent events would show, it proved to be disastrous for Churchill.

By this time some of Churchill's friends were beginning to agree with his critics, acknowledging his moments of brilliance but finding his actions increasingly unpredictable. Lloyd George, one of Churchill's closest political allies, said in private that he was becoming a liability to both the Government and the country. His past reputation, going back to Tonypandy and the Siege of Sidney Street, was not forgotten and his many enemies were waiting for him to make a crucial mistake. If he was aware of the clouds gathering around him, Churchill certainly didn't show it and he continued to run the Admiralty in what his critics described as his usual belligerent and over-bearing manner.

Gallipoli

The war on the Western Front quickly reached a stalemate, with the trenches dominated by artillery and machine gun fire. Any attempt to advance resulted in huge casualties and usually proved ineffective. In the first few months of 1915 Churchill attempted to finds ways of breaking this stalemate, which, if successful, would result in shortening the war. An example was Churchill's involvement in the development of the tank. When the idea of a landship, as it was then called[6], was brought to him at the Admiralty, he was immediately enthusiastic, initially seeing it as a way of transporting troops in safety rather than being the offensive weapon it would become. It was hardly the business of the Admiralty, but Churchill committed funding to a project which might otherwise have floundered. Tanks came into service in 1916, but were not hugely influential on the Western Front until 1918, when they were used en masse for the first time in a tactic advocated by Churchill.

Churchill was also engaged in the study of a wider strategy to shorten the war by opening fronts against the Central Powers other than the Western Front. He was particularly keen on a plan to land forces in northern Holland and the Baltic coast of Germany which could then strike at the interior of the country, perhaps even at Berlin itself. Another plan involved attacking Turkey in an attempt to knock it out of the war, followed by the opening of a front against Austro-Hungary through the Balkans. This initially involved a naval assault on the Turkish forts on the Gallipoli Peninsula which protected the approach to Constantinople through the narrow straits of the Dardanelles. With the forts knocked out, the navy could then force its way through the Dardanelles into the Sea of Marmara, from where it would be possible to bombard Constantinople which, it was generally assumed, would then quickly capitulate.

The strategy to be employed for the Dardanelles campaign was a source of much disagreement between the various members of the War Council, with both Churchill and Kitchener changing their minds on a number of occasions. The main area of disagreement concerned the question of whether the operation would need to be a combined one between the army and navy or could employ just the navy which alone would be sufficient to force the straits. Kitchener had a very low opinion of the Turkish Army and was certain they would abandon the Gallipoli Peninsula as soon as the forts came under naval bombardment. Churchill supported this view at first, but then decided that army landings would also be required to ensure the peninsula was taken. Fisher vacillated between, at one moment, extreme confidence in the navy's ability to succeed on its own and, at another, the desire to have nothing to do with the whole operation. His attitude only served to confuse the matter and caused a serious rift between him and Churchill who, along with others, was beginning to have doubts about Fisher's mental state.

Eventually Asquith decided that the operation was to go ahead as a combined operation, although Kitchener was reluctant to release the required number of troops. After further arguments it was finally decided to send an entire British division and the Australian and New Zealand Army Corps (ANZAC), then training in Egypt, together with a number of units of the French Army, the Royal Naval Division and smaller numbers of troops from around the Empire. Churchill and Fisher, who had suddenly changed his mind again and was enthusiastic about the plan, assembled a squadron of obsolete battleships, ones which it was felt could be risked in the minefields of the Dardanelles, together with the brand new Dreadnought-class battleship HMS *Queen Elizabeth* and various support ships and minesweepers.

The naval bombardment of the outer forts on the peninsula began towards the end of February and, although it was hampered by bad weather, it was perceived to have been successful. Intercepted German radio messages indicated that the forts were running low on ammunition, so it was decided to attempt to force the straits on 18 March, without waiting for the army which was not ready for a landing. Two days before the attack was to begin Admiral Carden, the commander of the squadron, had to step down because he was suffering from stress. He was replaced by Admiral de Robeck who, in communication with Churchill, assured him that he was as committed to a successful attack as his predecessor had been.

On 18 March, ten British and French battleships entered the straits to bombard the forts further along the coast of the Gallipoli Peninsula and were followed by minesweepers which would clear a path through the Dardanelles. The forts were quickly put out of action, to all intents and purposes, but a number of ships hit floating mines, including one French battleship which sank immediately with the loss of all 600 hands. The minesweepers were forced to withdraw and de Robeck decided to order a halt to the operation. Over the next few days, Churchill attempted to persuade him to renew the attack, arguing that the potential gain outweighed the risks involved, but de Robeck refused, having decided to wait until the army was ready. Churchill's advisers in the Admiralty, including Fisher, agreed with de Roebuck, so the naval attack was suspended for over a month while the landings on the peninsula were prepared. The Turkish Army used this time to prepare their defences, partly under the leadership of Mustafa Kemal who, under the name of Atatürk, would later become the founder and first President of modern Turkey.

From that point onwards the conduct of the campaign passed out of Churchill's hands. The landings on the peninsula and subsequent land battle came under the direction of Kitchener and the commander in the field, Sir Ian Hamilton, Churchill's old friend from the Boer War. The initial objectives of the first landings on 25 April[7] were to occupy the high ground on the interior of the peninsula which commanded the forts on the coast. After five days of fierce fighting the Allies had taken the cliff tops immediately behind the landing beaches but had not advanced any further, failing to reach any of the objectives set for them for the first day. The situation became increasingly chaotic, with poor communications a major factor contributing towards the failure. On one occasion a unit of British troops landed on a beach unopposed and advanced inland before the Turkish Army could mount a defence but then withdrew because they could not contact headquarters to establish what they were supposed to do after they had advanced.

As the land battle ground to a halt, Churchill and Fisher continued to argue about what the navy should do. On 15 May, Fisher resigned in a fit of pique after Churchill added two submarines to a list of naval reinforcements to be sent to the Dardanelles without consulting him. The Government was already under severe pressure after reports of a shortage of artillery shells on the Western Front had been published and, after Fisher resigned and with the Dardanelles going badly wrong, Bonar Law, the leader of the Conservative opposition, informed Asquith that the opposition would no longer adhere to the truce that had been agreed between the two parties and would challenge the Government in Parliament.

The crisis threatened Asquith's position as Prime Minister and, as a means of averting this, he invited the Conservatives to join a coalition Government, an offer which included representation on the War Council. Bonar Law accepted Asquith's proposal on the condition that Churchill was removed from the Admiralty, a price Asquith was willing to pay in order to preserve his own career. He appointed Churchill to the position of Chancellor of the Duchy of Lancaster, where he would continue to have a seat in the Cabinet but not one on the War Council. It also meant that he no longer had the authority of a Government ministry behind him so, although he was allowed to join the Dardanelles Committee, the newly-formed government body charged with overseeing the continuing campaign, his voice carried little weight.

There can be little doubt that Asquith was making Churchill the scapegoat for the disaster unfolding in the Dardanelles. As the Prime Minister who had ultimately authorised the campaign he was as culpable as Churchill and Kitchener, the Secretary of State for War, also bore a share of the responsibility for the conduct of the campaign. But it was Churchill who was effectively sacked and the stigma of failure was primarily attached to him. From then on, and for many years afterwards, wherever he made a public appearance he was greeted with cries of 'What about the Dardanelles?'. But, even though he was by no means solely responsible, he had made himself prominent in the planning and execution of the campaign and, had it been successful, he would have certainly taken the credit. In this way, at least, and also by making so many enemies throughout his political career by being so outspoken, he had set himself up for the fall. Even though he remained in the Cabinet, many commentators, particularly in the Conservative press, reached the conclusion that his political career was over at the age of forty.

Over the following months Churchill had little to do, since he had been frozen out of taking any further part in discussions by the Dardanelles Committee and barred from involvement in any other areas of government business by the Conservatives. He began to spend more time away from Westminster, going to stay in a farmhouse in the Surrey countryside. Inactivity always weighed heavily on him so, after encouragement from his sister-in-law Gwendeline and the artist Hazel Lavery, he took up painting to keep his mind occupied. With typical energy and enthusiasm, he applied himself to the task and, over the years, developed into a surprisingly proficient artist. During the Second World War he was to remark that he might not be a great painter but at least he was better than Hitler.

In August, the Gallipoli campaign was reinforced by further troop landings at Suvla Bay. However, the increased number of troops made little difference to the overall battle and the Allies were still pinned down in trenches. By October, the Dardanelles Committee was discussing plans to withdraw the troops from the peninsula. Churchill continued to support the campaign and, after the decision to evacuate the troops had been taken, he resigned from the Government with the intention of joining his territorial regiment, the Oxford Hussars, who were on active service in France.

The operation to evacuate the peninsula began in November and continued gradually over the next few months with very few casualties. It was, perhaps, the only successful operation of the entire campaign, although this hardly made amends for the disaster that had gone before. In all, the Allies suffered more than 200,000 casualties, with 43,000 men killed. Of these 21,000 were British, 10,000 French, 7,500 Australian and 2,700 from New Zealand. Not one of the original objectives of the campaign was achieved.

After the Fall

In deciding to join his regiment on the Western Front, Churchill was both paying a penance for the mistakes he had made and attempting to restore his reputation in the same way he had made it, by participating in military action. On arrival in France on 18 November, his old friend Sir John French, the

Commander-in-Chief of the British Expeditionary Force, offered him the command of a brigade and the rank of Brigadier-General, a very considerable step up from the rank of major he held in his own regiment. While waiting to find out which brigade he would be offered, he joined a Grenadier Guards division to gain experience of conditions in France. Within a few days of arriving in the country he was at the front, sheltering in a trench dugout from German artillery shells. Despite the discomfort and danger, he wrote to his wife, he was happier than he had been for many months.

On hearing of French's offer to Churchill, Asquith immediately vetoed it, aware that, if he allowed it to stand, he would face questions in the House of Commons about how Churchill's limited military experience could warrant his being offered such a high command. French had been called to London to be told he was being replaced as Commander-in-Chief of the BEF by Sir Douglas Haig. Referring to Churchill, Asquith now said to him, 'Perhaps you might give him a battalion'. Churchill reacted angrily to the dismissive tone of Asquith's words when he heard of them, writing to Clementine that he would do anything he could to hasten Asquith's demise as Prime Minister. He had been staying at French's headquarters in France but now, with Haig about to take over, he moved to the house not far away that Max Aitken (later Lord Beaverbrook) had taken in his official capacity as a Canadian observer of the Front. Aitken encouraged Churchill to consider a return to politics, cementing a friendship which, despite Aitken's sometimes disreputable reputation, lasted throughout their lives and would see Churchill offer Beaverbrook a position in his Cabinet during the Second World War.

At the beginning of January 1916, Churchill was offered the

command of the 6th Royal Scots Fusiliers, a battalion made up mostly of men from Argyll in Scotland which had suffered severe casualties at the First Battle of Ypres and was then being brought back up to strength with new recruits. Both officers and men were initially suspicious of Churchill, not helped by the first impression he made when he turned up with a mountain of luggage, including a large tin bath and a boiler for heating water. But he gained the respect and admiration of his men through a combination of energy and good sense in the training of the new recruits and a concern for the well-being of all the ranks. He was also quite lenient in dealing with minor infringements of army law and keen to organise sports and other entertainments.

After two weeks of training, the battalion moved up to the frontline, occupying 1,000 yards of trenches at the Belgium village of Ploegsteert, known as Plug Street in the army vernacular of the time, where they would alternately spend six days in the frontline and six days in reserve. Churchill divided his time between his headquarters in the village and a bombed-out farmhouse near the frontline. No major offensives occurred in his sector of the front during the three months he was there but there was a constant danger from artillery fire. Shells exploded near the farmhouse on numerous occasions and shrapnel injured officers inside it, although, with his usual luck under fire, Churchill remained unscathed.

Churchill's life at the front was made easier by regular supplies sent to him by Clementine, including Fortnum and Mason hampers and bottles of whisky and plum brandy. His wife's letters kept him informed about the political situation in the House of Commons and it was not long before he was itching to get back to London so he could participate in debates. He wrote about his desire to form an alternative Government to challenge Asquith, discussing his ideas with Lloyd George, Bonar Law and his close friend F E Smith (later Lord Birkenhead), who was then the Attorney General. They remained nothing more than points for discussion since none of these men appeared too keen on allying himself to Churchill at that time.

A brief return to London during a period of leave, in which he spoke in a debate in the House of Commons, further increased his enthusiasm for a return to politics, even though the rather bizarre call he made for the return of Lord Fisher to the Admiralty towards the end of his speech had been met with mockery in both parliament and the press. In May, his battalion was amalgamated with another and command was given to the senior officer in the other battalion. It gave Churchill the opportunity to return to London without giving the impression of abandoning his duties in the army. He wrote to Haig asking to be allowed to resume his political role and Haig agreed to let him leave the army. By 7 May he was back in the House of Commons but the shadow of the Dardanelles remained over him and this, together with continuing opposition from the Conservatives in the coalition Government, meant that there was no chance that he would be offered a ministerial office.

In a bid to clear his name, Churchill appealed to Asquith to allow him to publish the minutes of War Council meetings which would show the actual course of events in the Dardanelles campaign. Such a move would have been politically damaging to Asquith as the minutes would have exposed his own role in authorising the campaign and, unsurprisingly, he refused. In June, Kitchener, who had been increasingly sidelined after the Dardanelles, was drowned at sea when the ship that was taking him on a diplomatic mission to Russia hit a mine near the Orkneys and sank. Lloyd George became Secretary of State for War and Churchill briefly hoped that his old friend would exert his influence to get him back into Government. However, Lloyd George was not about to risk his own position by helping Churchill and the hopes came to nothing.

Towards the end of June, Churchill made a speech in the House of Commons in which he set out his opposition to frontal attacks on the Western Front and advocated various different strategies to take the war away from the trenches. A few days later, on 1 July, the Allied offensive began on the Somme, resulting in 57,000 casualties, including 19,000 killed, the largest number suffered by the British Army in a single day. The battle raged on throughout the summer and into the autumn, and the casualties continued to mount up, including Asquith's eldest son Raymond, who was killed in action in September. It finally ground to a halt in November, by which time the British and French forces had advanced about five miles.

In early December yet another crisis developed in the Cabinet, this time over the extent to which Asquith was attempting to interfere with Lloyd George's role as Secretary of State for War. A Cabinet rebellion against Asquith's premiership had been brewing for some time and, in order to force the issue, Lloyd George, Bonar Law and Lord Curzon, the Foreign Secretary, all resigned. It was a direct challenge to Asquith and left him with little option other than to resign himself, which he did with immediate effect. When Bonar Law failed in his attempt to form a Government, Lloyd George became Prime

Minister and immediately initiated a radical reorganisation, creating a smaller and more workable War Cabinet composed of those ministers who were directly responsible for the war effort. There was still no place for Churchill, who had been hoping Lloyd George would appoint him to the Air Ministry.

The Dardanelles Committee published its findings in March 1917 and, while making it clear that Churchill was not solely responsible for the disaster, it did not fully exonerate him from blame. Asquith and Kitchener were both criticised for their roles and the report also stated, in accordance with Churchill's view, that the initial naval attack would have stood a significant chance of success if it had been carried through with sufficient force. Even with his name at least partially cleared, it would be another three months before Churchill was offered a Government post by Lloyd George and then it was Minister of Munitions rather than Air Minister, meaning that he would not be involved in the War Cabinet and the day-to-day conduct of the war.

Almost two years after leaving office, when his career had appeared to be dead and buried, and despite the continuing opposition of the Conservatives, Churchill was back in Government. He immediately began to reorganise his department along more streamlined and efficient lines and instituted a committee which met every day to ensure that any problems and delays could be dealt with straight away. He also resolved a simmering industrial dispute and, in numerous trips to France, established a good working relationship with Haig, despite the criticisms he had made in Parliament of Haig's continuing faith that victory in the war overall would be achieved by frontal attacks on the Western Front.

The Americans joined the war in April 1917 and US Army

troops began to arrive in ever-increasing numbers. Churchill advocated a steady build-up in men and munitions, including tanks and aircraft, throughout the rest of 1917 and 1918, enough to ensure victory in 1919 without the disastrous frontal assaults that had previously proved so costly. As always he did not confine his thinking solely to the responsibilities of his department and, much to the annoyance of the Conservatives in the coalition Government, was frequently in contact with Lloyd George, who began to use him as an unofficial envoy between himself and the French Prime Minister Georges Clemenceau.

The Bolshevik Revolution in Russia in October 1917 resulted in the Russians signing an armistice with the Central Powers. This had the effect of freeing up the German troops on the Eastern Front for deployment in the west, although both armies were now so depleted of men that, had the Americans not joined, the war would surely have ground to a halt. The German Army launched an offensive in March 1918, hoping for a decisive breakthrough before the US Army was fully ready. It was almost successful, getting to within 75 miles of Paris before it was stopped. It would prove to be the last throw of the dice for the Germans who were forced into wholesale retreat after the Allies attacked at Amiens in August, breaking through with the aid of tanks. With morale falling apart in the retreating German Army and civil unrest developing at home, where the naval blockade had caused serious food shortages, an Allied victory now appeared to be only a matter of time.

By October, both the Ottoman Empire and the Austro-Hungarians had signed an armistice with the Allies, leaving Germany in an impossible and isolated position. On 7 November, a German delegation crossed the Allied lines under a flag of truce to ask for an armistice. They were escorted to a railway carriage in a siding in the Compiègne Forest where General Ferdinand Foch, the supreme commander of the Allied forces, and representatives from Britain and America put the terms of an armistice to them. The German delegation was forced to agree to the Allied terms, signing the armistice in the early hours of 11 November. The guns finally fell silent at eleven o'clock that morning.

At the time, Churchill was with Clementine in London at the Hotel Metropole, the building which had served as the base for the Ministry of Munitions. From his room he could hear Big Ben chiming the hour at eleven, later writing of the silence that occurred as the bell sounded and of the wild and chaotic celebrations that erupted immediately afterwards, with streams of people pouring out of buildings into the street. The two of them drove through the throngs of celebrating people to 10 Downing Street to congratulate Lloyd George who had already promised Churchill a ministerial position in the post-war Government.

Between the Wars

Secretary of State

In the immediate aftermath of the war Lloyd George, riding high on a wave of public popularity, called a general election which he fought as the leader of the coalition government established in 1916. Churchill stood again as the Liberal candidate for Dundee and won comfortably. The Government was returned to power with a huge majority. Churchill wanted to return to the Admiralty, perhaps seeing this as the final vindication of his reputation after it had been so badly damaged by the Dardanelles campaign, but Lloyd George offered him the joint ministerial position of Secretary of State for War and Air. By doing so, he presented Churchill with the immediate task of organising the demobilisation of more than three million men from the British Army in France.

Part of Churchill's demobilisation plan involved leaving a million men in the army in order to occupy the Rhineland region of Germany, which stretched along the border of France, Belgium and the Netherlands and was to become a demilitarised zone in accordance with the terms set out in the Treaty of Versailles. There can be little doubt that Churchill also wanted to maintain a large peacetime army in the event of a war with Bolshevik Russia, which he now considered to be a greater threat to peace in Europe than Germany. He advocated intervention in the developing civil war in Russia, in which the Red Army was fighting against a loose confederation of anti-Bolshevik forces collectively known as the White Russians. A force of 14,000 British soldiers had been sent to Russia in 1917 and was still there but Lloyd George, knowing that the British people had no stomach for another war, particularly one in the vast spaces of Russia, decided against any further intervention and the troops were withdrawn.

Over the next few years, Churchill became involved in a number of problems affecting British responsibilities overseas and, in January 1921, Lloyd George asked him to become Secretary of State for the Colonies in order to concentrate on these issues. It would be a difficult year for Churchill who would have to deal with three family bereavements as well as a heavy workload in government. In April, Clementine's brother William committed suicide. Shortly afterwards, Lady Randolph fell on a flight of stairs and broke her ankle. Gangrene developed in her leg and it was amputated above the knee but she suffered a haemorrhage in an artery in her thigh a few days after the operation and, at the age of 67, she died. As if this was not enough, Churchill's daughter Marigold caught a cold in August which developed into septicaemia and this led to her death on the twenty-third of that month.

One of the main issues Churchill had to deal with on becoming Colonial Secretary was what to do with the former Ottoman territories of Mesopotamia and Palestine, both of which had become British mandates in 1920 under the terms of the Treaty of Sèvres, the final settlement between the Allies and the Ottomans. The root of the problems went back to promises made by the British to Arab leaders during the First World War in order to induce them to revolt against the

Ottomans which appeared to guarantee the creation of a continuous Arab state throughout much of the region.

T E Lawrence, who was involved in the Arab revolt and became known as Lawrence of Arabia, supported the Arab cause but, even before the First World War was over, the promises made by the British Government had been undermined. The Sykes-Picot Agreement, made in secret between the British and French in 1916, detailed how the region would be divided up between them after the war. Only the area which now forms Saudi Arabia was to be given to the Arabs, largely because it was then thought to be made up of useless expanses of sand. In the case of Palestine, British promises were further undermined by the Balfour Declaration of 1917, a letter to British Jews written by Arthur Balfour, Foreign Secretary at the time, which contained a formal statement of support for the Zionist aspiration of establishing what the declaration described as 'a natural home for the Jewish people' in Palestine.

Churchill considered the maintenance of British forces in the region to deal with local insurrections to be prohibitively expensive and it was at this time, according to his detractors at least, that he advocated using the RAF to drop gas bombs on tribesmen in Iraq. Documents from the period actually show that he was suggesting the use of a form of tear gas to disperse groups of militants without causing them permanent harm rather than any kind of poison gas. However, inaccurate though it may be, the idea that he wished to kill Arab tribesmen with poison gas stuck to his name and is still repeated today.

As a means of finding ways of sorting out the problems in the British mandates, and of reducing the cost of governing them, Churchill convened a conference in Cairo in March 1921 which was attended by the British administrators of the regions. Lawrence was there in his capacity as Churchill's Middle East advisor and, together with Gertrude Bell, who had been instrumental in drawing up the boundaries of what is now Iraq, persuaded Churchill to offer Faisal bin Hussein, the leader of the Arab Revolt and son of the Sharif of Mecca, the monarchy of this newly constituted country. Faisal's brother Abdullah was also offered a monarchy, becoming the King of Transjordan, the area of the Palestinian mandate east of the Jordan river.[8] After the conference Churchill travelled to Jerusalem, where he attempted to placate the Palestinians who were protesting about Jewish immigration into the region, although he remained in favour of the eventual creation of a Jewish state.

The other major task facing Churchill was finding a solution to the perennial problem of Irish Home Rule. This had been put on hold at the start of the First World War but, as the Easter Rising in Dublin in 1916 had shown, the situation in Ireland remained volatile and needed to be resolved. In the General Election of 1919, the republican Sinn Fein party had won almost all of the seats in Ireland outside Ulster. Rather than take up their seats in Westminster, the newly-elected Sinn Fein MPs constituted a parliament in Dublin, which was not recognised by Britain. As a consequence the Irish Republican Army, in which Michael Collins played a leading role, began a guerrilla war against the British presence in Ireland, including acts of sabotage, kidnapping and murder.

The British response, initiated by Lloyd George and supported by Churchill, was to send to Ireland two newly-formed military units, made up of unemployed ex-servicemen, in an attempt to stop the violence. They became known as the

Auxis, a shortened version of Auxiliaries, and the Black and Tans, after the mixed police and army uniforms they wore. They quickly gained a notorious reputation in Ireland for the brutal methods they employed, carrying out reprisals for IRA actions against republican targets which included murder and the burning of villages.

The brutality of the Auxis and Black and Tans only served to escalate the violence and, in July 1921, Lloyd George called for a ceasefire. In the truce that followed, negotiations began in London between the two sides, the principal figures in the talks being Lloyd George and Churchill for the British Government and Arthur Griffith and Michael Collins for the Irish. Churchill was mostly concerned with the military aspects of the subsequent treaty which he negotiated with Michael Collins. The two of them established a good working relationship and, after the Anglo-Irish Treaty was signed in December, Collins wrote to Churchill on a number of occasions to thank him for his help. However, he also said that, in signing the treaty, he felt as if he had been signing his own death warrant.

The treaty established the Irish Free State, an independent entity with Dominion status within the British Empire. It also made provision for Northern Ireland, already partitioned by an Act of Parliament, to opt out of the Irish Free State, leading to the creation of a boundary commission to establish the border between Northern Ireland and the Free State. The main military provisions in the treaty allowed Britain to retain control of three ports on the west coast of Ireland, which became known as the Treaty Ports[9], so that they could continue to be used by the Royal Navy.

The Anglo-Irish treaty caused a deep division in Ireland. Michael Collins considered it to be one step on the road to

Ireland becoming a republic but other members of Sinn Fein and the IRA refused to accept a compromise deal with the British. A civil war broke out between those factions supporting the treaty and those who opposed it. Collins, as he had predicted, was killed in August 1922 during an ambush in County Cork by anti-Treaty IRA men. The pro-Treaty IRA won the civil war in the following year but the divisions created during the bitter and bloody struggle would be evident in Ireland for many years to come.

Throughout this period, and on into the summer of 1922, Greece and Turkey were engaged in a war over the territory, extending through the European part of Turkey and into Anatolia, which Greece had been awarded in the Treaty of Sèvres. It was a dirty war in which both sides committed atrocities against civilians. Lloyd George was strongly in favour of Greece but Turkish nationalists, under the command of Mustafa Kemal, gained the upper hand and gradually pushed the Greek army out of what they regarded as their homeland. In September 1922, the Turkish army began to threaten the British base at Chanak (known as Çanakkale in Turkey) which had been established under the terms of the treaty to guard the neutral zone of the Dardanelles Straits. Lloyd George and Churchill advocated a strong show of force and, for a short period, the prospect of war with Turkey became a very real one.

The Chanak Crisis, as it came to be called, quickly fizzled out but it was to prove the final straw for the Conservatives, the largest group in the Coalition Government, when it came to co-operation with Lloyd George. He had also been caught selling honours, including peerages and knighthoods, and, although he was not actually prosecuted, his sleazy actions hardly inspired confidence. At what would become a famous meeting of the Carlton Club, a gentlemen's club in London with long-standing links to the Conservative Party, a decision was taken by Conservative MPs to withdraw from the coalition with Lloyd George's Liberals and to fight the next general election as an independent party. This decision forced Lloyd George to resign as Prime Minister and, although he would remain in Parliament as a Liberal MP until his death in 1945, he never again held any ministerial position in Government.

As the leader of the Conservative Party, Bonar Law became Prime Minister and immediately called a general election. Churchill had been suffering from appendicitis as the coalition unravelled and was recovering from the subsequent operation as the election approached, which prevented him from campaigning in his Dundee constituency until a week before the vote. He would use this as an excuse when he lost his seat to the Labour candidate but, in truth, the country had turned against Lloyd George after four years of post-war governance which had been marked by continuing economic problems. The Liberals were comprehensively defeated and Labour became the second largest party in the country for the first time. Writing about the experience of losing his seat some years later, Churchill said, 'In the twinkling of an eye I found myself without an office, without a seat, without a party and without an appendix'. But at the time he was far less flippant. He was then 48 years old and, after 22 years as an MP, he found himself suddenly without a job.

In the immediate aftermath of the defeat Churchill left for his regular holiday destination of the South of France, taking Clementine and the children, including the newly arrived Mary, with him. He spent his time painting and writing what would become *The World Crisis*, the book he had begun the previous year which mixed the history of the First World War with his own experiences of the conflict. At the time the South of France was the favoured place for winter holidays for many of the upper echelons of British society and, somewhat to Clementine's annoyance, Churchill spent a good deal of his time drinking with his friends and gambling at the casino in Monte Carlo.

Re-ratting

After more than a year out of politics and with his enthusiasm for public life apparently restored, Churchill stood as the Liberal candidate for Leicester West in the general election of December 1923 and was once again defeated. The Liberal Party, with an uneasy truce declared between Lloyd George and Asquith, joined a coalition with Labour under the leadership of Ramsay MacDonald to form a government. Since Churchill continued to maintain his fervent dislike for anything to do with socialism, this can be regarded as the moment when his association with the Liberal Party came to an end. His old Conservative opponent Bonar Law died of cancer shortly before the election and Stanley Baldwin, who was more sympathetic towards Churchill, took over as leader but Conservative policies on protectionism were an obstacle to Churchill rejoining the party immediately since he remained very much in favour of free trade.

The coalition between the Liberals and Labour was highly unstable and, after a motion of no confidence was passed in September 1924, it fell apart. Another general election was called for the following month. Baldwin offered Churchill the safe Conservative seat of Epping, which he accepted, standing as what he described as an independent 'Constitutionalist' candidate rather than as a Conservative. He won the seat comfortably and, with the Conservatives returned with a large majority, he thought Baldwin might offer him a Government position in one of the ministries he had worked in before, such as the Admiralty or the Colonial Office. Much to his surprise, and to that of many in the Conservative Party, Baldwin asked him if he would consider the position of Chancellor of the Exchequer. This was a question to which, he would later write, he had wanted to reply, 'Will the bloody duck swim?', but, in consideration of the gravity of the moment, what he actually said was, 'I shall be proud to serve you in this splendid Office.'

At first sight Churchill was not an obvious candidate for Chancellor of the Exchequer, the office with overall responsibility for the economic and financial affairs of the country. He could barely manage his own finances, regularly spending more than his income and incurring large debts. But the appointment was, to a certain extent, a political one, with Baldwin taking a calculated gamble by offering the job to Churchill in an effort both to drive a wedge between him and Lloyd George and to encourage him to rejoin the Conservative party.

In the following year Churchill actually did rejoin the party, commenting at the time, 'Anyone can rat, but it takes a certain ingenuity to re-rat'. By this time, the opinions of his many detractors were so firmly entrenched that the actual circumstances hardly mattered. According to them he was an opportunist who had rejoined the Conservatives only after it had become apparent that the Liberals were a spent political force, thus confirming the fact that he lacked principles and could not be trusted. But even his harshest critics could recognise his talents, on occasion describing him as 'mercurial' and as having 'a zig-zag streak of lightning in his brain'. He could have flashes of brilliance and was an inspirational speaker, capable of turning the House of Commons in favour of his argument with the force of his rhetoric. Yet these same qualities could have dangerous consequences because of the unreliable nature of policies which resulted from them.

At the age of fifty, Churchill was as energetic as he had ever been, shaking up the civil servants in the Treasury with a steady stream of instructions and questions in the form of written minutes. In his first few months as Chancellor he worked closely with Neville Chamberlain, then the Minister for Health, on a raft of social measures, including the extension of the system of national insurance and reforms to pensions for the old and widows which echoed his concerns as a minister in the Liberal Government before the First World War. He also made great progress in untangling the web of international debts left over from the war and worked towards limiting military expenditure, particularly at the Admiralty. But without a doubt the most important issue he had to deal with was whether or not to restore Britain to the gold standard. This was the exchange mechanism that had been in place before the First World War but which had been suspended in 1914 in order to fund military spending.

The Biggest Mistake

Churchill inherited the policy of returning to the gold standard from his predecessor at the Exchequer but it was now his responsibility to make the final decision. He instigated a debate on the subject, with Montagu Norman, the Governor of the

Bank of England, and Otto Niemeyer, the Controller of Finance at the Treasury, arguing in favour of a return, and the highly respected and influential economist John Maynard Keynes and Churchill's old friend Lord Beaverbrook against, both adamant that it would result in deflation and unemployment.

In response to the conflicting advice he received, Churchill eventually accepted the views expressed by the Treasury and the Bank of England and, in his budget speech in May 1925, announced that Britain would be returning to the gold standard, a move which resulted in sterling being revalued upwards to its pre-war exchange rate with the dollar of one pound to $4.86. In later years, Churchill would reflect that this had been the biggest mistake of his life and that Keynes had been right about the consequences of such a move. It resulted in British exports becoming significantly more expensive, and there was a consequent decline in overseas orders for much of the country's major industries, including shipbuilding, cotton milling and steel making. Coalmining was hit particularly hard, with coal supplies from competing countries becoming significantly cheaper, thus leading mine owners to attempt to impose wage cuts on miners in order to maintain their profits. This inevitably caused industrial dispute and mining unions threatened to strike unless the prospects of wage cuts were withdrawn. The Government offered the industry a subsidy to make up wages, averting a strike in 1925, but no agreement had been reached by the time the subsidy ran out in March of the following year and the miners walked out.

At the beginning of May 1926, the General Council of the Trades Union Congress called a general strike of all its affiliated members, resulting in three million men striking and almost all of Britain's industry and transport coming to a halt. Churchill regarded the miners' strike as a legitimate industrial dispute but he considered the general strike to be a constitutional challenge to Britain which had to be countered. He became increasingly bellicose in his rhetoric, seeing Bolshevik agitation everywhere and warning of civil war and revolution. He advocated the use of the army, including tanks and machine guns if necessary, to protect food supplies coming into the country, a move widely seen as a huge overreaction to the situation. Baldwin put him in charge of producing a Government newspaper, the *British Gazette*, ostensibly to keep the country informed in the absence of regular newspapers while the printers were on strike, but perhaps also to keep him occupied and out of trouble.

The strike lasted ten days before the TUC brought it to an end after a meeting with the Government, even though they received none of the guarantees they sought to prevent any of the strikers being victimised by their employers. The miners remained out until November, when poverty forced many of them back to work. Churchill, already vilified by the left in general, was blamed by many in the union movement for Government policy blatantly favouring the ruling classes. In truth, he may have fiercely opposed the general strike but he had favoured a negotiated settlement with the miners which addressed their legitimate grievances. As usual with Churchill, the prominence of his voice on the issue caused him to be regarded as the main protagonist when, in reality, this was not entirely the case.

Into the Wilderness

The hard line approach Churchill had taken over the general strike and his fervent opposition towards socialism in general dissipated much of the antipathy towards him from many in the Conservative Party. Over the next few years he remained as Chancellor of the Exchequer and was even spoken of, in the same way as Neville Chamberlain often was, as a possible successor to Baldwin as leader of the party. With unemployment continuing to rise as the economic situation declined, the Baldwin government began to run out of steam. As the next general election, in May 1929, approached, it became increasingly apparent that the Conservatives were losing the support of the country.

Churchill was returned in the Epping seat but, as predicted, the Labour Party won the most seats. Although they didn't have an overall majority in Parliament, Ramsay MacDonald formed his second administration, with Lloyd George's Liberals winning forty seats and holding the balance of power. Churchill took up his position on the opposition front benches, beginning a ten-year period in which he did not hold any official position, now often referred to as his 'wilderness years'. This is usually portrayed as the time when he became an isolated figure who spent most of his days building walls in his garden at Chartwell, the house he had bought in the Kent countryside in 1922. There is an element of truth in this portrayal in that he had developed an interest in landscape gardening and found bricklaying a distraction from politics, but he also remained active in parliament, taking part in numerous debates and often being consulted by government ministers on matters concerning military affairs. He was also regularly given privileged access to information not available to most backbench MPs, so he remained an influential voice in parliament.

Immediately after the election defeat, Churchill began to make extensive plans for future writing projects. He had recently established a system of writing involving the use of research assistants and dictation to his secretary which vastly increased his literary output and which enabled him to finish the last volumes of *The World Crisis* and *My Early Life*. Now he began to plan a book on his illustrious ancestor John Churchill, the first Duke of Marlborough, and his cousin Sunny made available to him previously unpublished documents held at Blenheim Palace. All these books, together with a bewildering array of articles for various newspapers and magazines, together with the services of a good agent, made him one of the highest earning authors in Britain at that time.

Before beginning his book on Marlborough, Churchill embarked on an extensive tour of Canada and the USA, accompanied by his son Randolph, now eighteen years old, his brother Jack and Jack's son Johnny. The tour lasted for almost four months and, for much of the time, they travelled in a private railway carriage put at their disposal by a wealthy Canadian railway magnate. During the course of their travels, Churchill had dinner with Charlie Chaplin in Hollywood and was a guest of William Randolph Hearst at his palatial castle in California. He also visited the Grand Canyon and the battle-fields of the American Civil War, before arriving in New York at exactly the moment of the Wall Street Crash on Black Tuesday, 29 October 1929, the event which would signal the beginning of the Great Depression of the early 1930s.

Churchill had invested much of his literary earnings in stocks and shares and lost in excess of £10,000 himself (about £250,000 today) in the crash. The following day he witnessed from the window of his apartment, which overlooked Wall Street, the human cost of the crash, writing, 'Under my window a gentleman cast himself down fifteen storeys and was dashed to pieces, causing a wild commotion and the arrival of the fire brigade'.

The loss of so much of his earnings would cause him some financial hardship over the next few years but his experiences in the US renewed his faith in the necessity of a strong bond between Britain and America. Two years later he returned to the country on a speaking tour which got off to a disastrous start after he was hit by a car while attempting to cross Fifth Avenue in New York. Without thinking where he was, he had looked left before stepping into the road, as he would normally do in Britain, and was hit by a car coming from the right. No bones were broken but he was badly injured and, as he was now 57, it took him a month to recover sufficiently to begin his speaking engagements. Over the next three weeks he took a percentage of the income from each venue and thus earned £7,500, which was considerably more than his salary had been as Chancellor of the Exchequer.

Finding a Cause

The differences between Churchill and his colleagues in the Conservative Business Committee, as the Shadow Cabinet was then known, deepened throughout 1930. As the Great Depression took hold, Baldwin began to favour a limited form of protectionism, very much against Churchill's long held support for free trade. But, despite these differences, this was not the issue which caused the final split between Churchill and Baldwin. That came over Baldwin's support of the Labour

Government's policy on Indian Home Rule which involved devising a plan to grant the country the status of a Dominion within the Empire.

Churchill's view of India remained firmly based on the imperial assumption of the benefits brought to the country by inclusion in the Empire. His opinions had changed little since he had been stationed in Bangalore with his cavalry regiment in the 1890s, when he had taken more interest in playing polo than in the country. He adopted the patronising, and not a little racist, attitude that the people of India were incapable of governing themselves. But at the heart of his opposition was the realisation that, in granting Home Rule, a step would have been taken towards full independence and, since other countries would undoubtedly follow India's lead, this would effectively mark the end of the British Empire.

In January 1931, Churchill resigned from the Shadow Cabinet. He would not hold another position while Baldwin remained leader of the Conservative Party. The continuing economic crisis also opened divisions in the Labour Government. Arguments raged over whether they should attempt to balance the budget by cutting public spending, as Ramsay MacDonald advocated, or to adopt the model developed by John Maynard Keynes of intervention in the economy in an attempt to stimulate it. These divisions proved impossible to resolve and MacDonald resigned as Prime Minister in August 1931. In a move which would ruin his reputation in the Labour movement, he then invited the Conservatives and Liberals to form a coalition National Government. Churchill, who was on holiday in France at the time, was not offered a position in the new Government, which was dominated by the Conservatives. MacDonald was already showing signs of the ill health which would force him to resign in 1935 and, although he continued as Prime Minister, Baldwin and Chamberlain were effectively running the country.

With his isolation from the leadership of the Conservative Party, Churchill had no prospect of gaining a position of any power in Government for the foreseeable future. His stance on India was only supported by a limited number of Conservative backbenchers, known as the Die-hards, mostly MPs from the right of the party who had previously been amongst his fiercest critics. And he could say little on the disastrous state of the economy because his decision to return to the gold standard in 1925 was widely perceived to have been a significant factor in contributing to the severity of the depression. What he needed was to find a cause which would allow him to remain in the public eye while he was not a member of the Government so that, should the opportunity arise, he would be in a position to make another comeback.

Early in 1932, Churchill began to make speeches and to write articles in the newspapers which warned of the danger to peace in Europe posed by the rise of Adolf Hitler and the Nazi Party in Germany. To say that he did this solely for his own political ends is by no means accurate. There can be no doubt that he recognised the brutality and openly anti-Semitic nature of Nazism right from the start. None the less, in opposing the response of the British Government to Hitler, he had found his cause, although, at least at first, this did not necessarily mean he was completely opposed to fascism in general. He was not overly critical of Mussolini's rise to power in Italy nor did he regard Japan as posing any great threat to British interests in the Far East after it had annexed Manchuria in 1931, an opinion which would later appear to be badly misjudged.

In August 1932, Churchill set off on a trip to Germany, ostensibly to visit the Blenheim battlefield in Bavaria as research for his book on Marlborough, but also to take the chance to assess the situation in Germany for himself. While he was in Munich he met Ernst 'Putzi' Hanfstaengl, an acquaintance of his son Randolph who was also a close friend of Hitler. Hanfstaengl suggested a meeting between Churchill and Hitler which, had it happened, would have been the only time the two future adversaries met in person. Churchill agreed to the meeting but Hitler, possibly put off by Churchill's disapproval of Nazi anti-Semitism, declined the opportunity.

The Storm Approaches

With the benefit of hindsight, the British government's policy of disarmament in the middle years of the 1930s now appears to be fundamentally flawed, and Churchill's argument of diplomacy from a position of strength has been entirely vindicated. The actual situation at the time was more complicated. All the major powers advocated the use of diplomacy to settle disputes between countries through the League of Nations, the international organisation set up after the First World War in the hope of providing a way in which future wars could be avoided. The Geneva Disarmament Conferences, beginning in 1932, aimed at preventing another arms race of the kind considered to have been a major cause of the conflict in 1914.

The harsh conditions imposed on Germany in the Treaty of Versailles, particularly the payment of vast and completely unrealistic reparations, were partly responsible for the severity of the Depression in Germany, when rampant inflation and mass unemployment destroyed the economy. In such dire circumstances, the extreme nationalism of the Nazi Party flourished, and it grew from a relatively small and localised fascist movement centred on Munich in the 1920s to become the largest political party in Germany after 1930. In January 1933, this led to Hitler becoming Chancellor of Germany.

Hitler's intentions soon became clear as he put in place measures to transform Germany into a one-party state. In the so-called Night of the Long Knives, towards the end of June that year, he concentrated power in his own hands by having dissenting members of his own party murdered. On the death of Hindenburg in August, he became Head of State, giving himself the title of *Führer*, and assuming the supreme command of the German armed forces. Shortly afterwards Germany withdrew from the Geneva Disarmament Conference and, in the following year, from the League of Nations. If his intentions from these actions were not clear enough, Hitler had openly stated his political philosophy in *Mein Kampf* (*My Struggle*), the book he had written while serving a jail sentence in 1924 after the abortive Beer Hall Putsch in Munich the previous year. It spelled out his ideas on *lebensraum* (literally 'living space') which detailed his ambition of territorial expansion for the German people in the east, and made clear the anti-Semitism which underpinned almost all of his thinking.

In both his actions and his writing, Hitler had set out exactly what he wanted to achieve so there should have been no excuse for politicians in Britain and the rest of the world to ignore Churchill's warnings. As it was, there was no desire amongst almost any other MP in the House of Commons to take any measures which might provoke war. It was perhaps under-standable only fifteen years after the end of the First World War but it was also indefensible when Germany's extensive programme of rearmament, undertaken in direct contravention of the Treaty of Versailles, became clear during the course of 1934. Despite this knowledge the British Government continued to follow a policy of disarmament. This was vigorously opposed by Churchill who began a vociferous campaign to expand the Royal Air Force with the aim of maintaining parity with the Luftwaffe.

In the following year, Baldwin took over as Prime Minister and, in November, the National Government won a landslide victory in what would prove to be the last general election held in Britain before 1945. It strengthened Baldwin's position enormously, making Churchill less of a threat to him. Churchill was brought in from the cold to a limited extent and was invited to serve on a number of Government committees and to advise on defence issues. However, there was still no place for him in a permanent position. More money was made available for the air force and the navy, although the army continued to be cut back, but Churchill perceived it to be a slow and uncommitted effort.

In March 1936, the German army entered the demilitarised zone of the Rhineland in a further contravention of the Treaty of Versailles. The response of both Britain and France was weak, as it had been to Italy's invasion of Abyssinia (now Ethiopia) in the previous year. Both countries advocated the use of diplomacy to resolve the issue which, in effect, allowed the Germans to march into the region unopposed. For once, Churchill was relatively restrained in his response, regarding the League of Nations as representing a united front which guaranteed the security of its members.

In a speech to the House of Commons made in November and aimed mainly at Baldwin, Churchill was highly critical of the lack of effort the Government had shown in rearmament, which had allowed Germany to get a head start of more than two years. He proposed that a new Ministry of Supply should be set up to ensure military procurement was not held up, describing those in Government who were responsible for the lack of action as having 'decided only to be undecided, resolved to be irresolute, adamant for drift, solid for fluidity, all power-ful to be impotent'. He ended the speech in typically emphatic terms:

> I have been staggered by the failure of the House of Commons to react effectively against those dangers [posed by German rearmament]. That, I am bound to say, I never expected. I never would have believed that we should have been allowed to go on getting into this plight, month by month, year by year, and that even the Government's own confessions of error would have produced no concentration of Parliamentary opinion and force capable of lifting our efforts to the level of emergency. I say that unless the House resolves to find out the truth for itself it will have committed an act of abdication of duty without parallel in its long history.

The speech itself was devastating enough but Baldwin's reply could have been fatal to his premiership. He explained that he had not taken sufficient action to rearm because, had he done so, pacifist feeling in the country was such that he believed he would have lost the 1935 election. Churchill would later write, 'That a Prime Minister should avow that he had not done his duty in regard to national safety because he was afraid of losing the election was an incident without parallel in our Parliamentary history'.

However, at exactly the moment Churchill appeared to be

finally winning the debate, the constitutional crisis surrounding King Edward VIII's expressed intention to marry the twice-divorced American Wallis Simpson intervened. Churchill had been a personal friend of Edward for many years and, although his advice was not to proceed with the marriage, he nevertheless supported the King. Baldwin was determined to end the matter, perhaps as a distraction from the problems he was having in the House of Commons, and, on his initiative, the King was presented with an ultimatum. He had to give up the idea of the marriage or abdicate. With Edward appearing to favour abdication, Churchill attempted to persuade the Government to allow the King to have more time to consider his decision, hoping that he would change his mind. On putting his opinions to the House of Commons, he found himself shouted down, having badly misjudged the mood of most MPs. A rumour began that those MPs who supported Edward were organising a King's Party to challenge the Government and that the party was to be led by Churchill. The rumour proved to be completely unfounded, but the damage had been done.

The King formally abdicated on 11 December, and was replaced by his brother Albert, who was crowned as King George VI the following May. The momentum that had been gathering behind the idea of Churchill's return to Government had been lost and, when Baldwin retired shortly after George VI's coronation, Neville Chamberlain was elected as leader of the Conservative Party. Since he was the leader of the largest party in the National Government, he also became the next Prime Minister.

History has not been kind to Chamberlain but he was widely regarded as the best man for the job of Prime Minister at an extremely difficult time and as a much safer pair of hands to deal with the escalating international situation than Churchill. He is now the man most closely associated with the policy of appeasement which, at that time, implied looking for diplomatic solutions to problems arising between countries through negotiation and compromise. Only later did the word acquire the connotations it has today of attempting to placate an aggressor by allowing them to do whatever they want. Appeasement turned out to be an entirely ineffective way of dealing with the menace of Nazi Germany. Chamberlain's fatal mistake was to assume that it was possible to deal with Hitler by diplomatic means alone and that Hitler would honour the negotiated agreements he made. What Hitler actually concluded from appeasement was that Britain would not go to war with Germany no matter what he did in Europe, as long as his actions didn't impinge on British interests anywhere else in the world. In this way, rather than prevent war, Chamberlain's efforts actually encouraged Hitler to believe he could dominate continental Europe.

The first challenging international problem for Chamberlain came only a few months after he became Prime Minister. In March 1938, Austria was incorporated into Nazi Germany in what has become known as the *Anschluss*. There was considerable support for the Nazi regime within the country and most Austrians put up little resistance to this but it was the first time the German army had crossed an international border since the First World War and can be seen as the first step towards Hitler's aim of creating a German Empire within Europe. Chamberlain's response was muted, in line with the policy of appeasement, and also because he recognised that there was little Britain could do about it without the use of force. Churchill was sympathetic, recognising the difficult position Chamberlain had inherited, but he continued to issue warnings about the gravity of the situation, saying in the House of Commons, 'Europe is confronted with a programme of aggression, nicely calculated and timed, unfolding stage by stage'.

His remarks were borne out by events, with Hitler's attention turning immediately to the Sudetenland, a region of Czechoslovakia adjoining the German and Austrian borders where there was a large population of ethnically German people. The threat of a German invasion of Czechoslovakian territory increased over the summer, as German forces built up along the border. The French had previously signed a treaty with Czechoslovakia, guaranteeing their independence, so an invasion looked as if it would lead directly to a European war. Chamberlain flew to Germany on three separate occasions to negotiate directly with Hitler in an effort to avert war. In the first two of these meetings he agreed to the cession of the Sudetenland to Germany without consulting the Czechoslovakian Government. Hitler's response to getting his own way, and to what he perceived as Chamberlain's weakness, was to declare his intention of occupying the region with the German army.

The third meeting occurred on 29 September at a conference held in Munich which was also attended by Mussolini and by Édouard Daladier, the Prime Minister of France. A Czechoslovakian delegation had travelled to the city but its members were not allowed to participate in the discussions to decide the fate of their country, which soon resulted in an agreement to allow the German occupation. A resolution was signed by all four participants to this effect and Chamberlain returned to Britain the next day to receive a hero's reception at Heston Aerodrome where he famously held the agreement up above his head to show it to the gathered crowd. Later that day he described the Munich Agreement as representing 'peace for our time', a view shared by the majority of MPs, but very definitely not by Churchill. A few days later he described the agreement as 'a total and unmitigated defeat' which had compromised Czechoslovakia's ability to defend itself against further incursions into its territory which, he thought, would only be a matter of months away. The British people, Churchill continued, should know the truth of the situation, saying:

> They should know that there has been gross neglect and deficiency in our defences; they should know that we have sustained a defeat without a war, the consequences of which will travel far with us along our road; they should know that we have passed an awful milestone in our history, when the whole equilibrium of Europe has been deranged, and the terrible words have been pronounced against the Western democracies: 'Thou art weighed in the balance and found wanting.' And do not suppose that this is the end. This is only the beginning of the reckoning. This is only the first sip, the first foretaste of a bitter cup which will be proffered to us year by year unless by a supreme recovery of moral health and martial vigour, we arise again and take our stand for freedom as in the olden time.

It was a devastating indictment of the agreement and, like so many of Churchill's speeches from that time, remains powerful today, not least because what he said was borne out by subsequent events. But it had little impact on the overwhelming majority of MPs in the House of Commons, who remained firmly in favour of the agreement. Churchill was now more isolated than he had ever been, only retaining the support of a handful of friends, and he received criticism from all sides. As ridiculous as it now appears, he was even accused by Hitler of being a warmonger.

On 15 March 1939, German troops entered Prague and shortly afterwards Czechoslovakia effectively ceased to exist, being partitioned between Germany and the Nazi client state of Slovakia. Hitler immediately turned his attention towards Poland, demanding that a strip of territory known as the Polish Corridor, which ran along the Baltic coast of the country and included the port city of Danzig (now Gdansk), should be ceded to Germany to link it with the German enclave of East Prussia. By this time Chamberlain, having finally come to realise that the Munich Agreement was a sham, had issued a guarantee to Poland, offering it military assistance if it was attacked.

Hitler increased the diplomatic pressure on Poland to acquiesce to his demands and, on 23 August, Germany signed the Molotov-Ribbentrop Pact with Russia, a treaty of non-aggression between the two countries which also contained secret sections detailing how Central Europe, including Poland, would be divided up between the two countries. The British response was to formalise its guarantee to Poland, joining France in signing a treaty of military assistance on 25 August. Hitler had planned to launch an invasion on the following day but he postponed it at the last moment on hearing of the British and French treaty.

The delay didn't last long. On 31 August, German troops wearing Polish Army uniforms staged an attack on a radio station near the Polish border and this was used as a pretext for the invasion of Poland which began the next day. After two days of vacillating, exacerbated while he waited for the French

Government to make up its mind what to do, Chamberlain sent an ultimatum to Germany at 9 o'clock in the morning of 3 September, demanding an immediate halt to the invasion and the withdrawal of German forces, with a deadline set at 11 o'clock for a response. No reply was received and, as Chamberlain said in a radio announcement to the nation made at 11.15 that day, 'consequently this country is at war with Germany'.

War Leader

Winston is Back

Churchill's isolation from the Conservative leadership, and the fact that he had been excluded from the National Government for almost ten years by the time war was declared in September 1939, worked in his favour in the spring and summer of that year. He was one of the few prominent British politicians whose reputation was not tarnished by association with either disarmament or appeasement. Sections of the press had been campaigning for his inclusion in the Cabinet for some months and, two days before Britain declared war on Germany, Chamberlain had finally offered him a position in the forth-coming War Cabinet, although he did not specify what it would be. Churchill reacted with impatience and was described as pacing around his flat in Morpeth Mansions like a caged lion as he waited to hear what post he would be given.

On the afternoon of 3 September, Churchill finally met Chamberlain who had decided to offer him the post of First Lord of the Admiralty, the same job he had held at the beginning of the First World War and had been forced to leave in the aftermath of the Dardanelles campaign. He immediately sent a telegram to the Admiralty to tell them he would be starting work later that day, prompting a signal to be sent out to the fleet which simply said, 'Winston is back'.

The initial stages of the war are now often known as the Phoney War because there was little armed contact between the opponents on land. What fighting there was occurred almost exclusively at sea, which served to keep Churchill's name in the forefront of the minds of MPs and the British public. Chamberlain's reserved and urbane manner, which had been one of the reasons he had been so successful as a politician, hardly appeared suitable for the conduct of a war. The energy and conviction which Churchill put into his speeches in the House of Commons and in radio broadcasts began to eclipse the Prime Minister, and soon many people expected him to become leader of the war effort in the near future.

In the meantime, Churchill set about his work in the Admiralty with his usual vigour, converting most of those there who had been sceptical about his appointment, including Sir Dudley Pound, the First Sea Lord, into ardent admirers. Many of the practices which would later become such a feature of his war leadership were initiated at this time, building on his vast experience of ministerial Government in the past. He could be idiosyncratic and, at times, impatient, demanding immediate responses to the huge number of instructions and inquiries he made every day in the form of written minutes, particularly those he had labelled in red with the words 'Action this Day' to indicate their urgency.

Churchill structured his day so that he could fit in as much work as possible. He often began in bed at about 8 o'clock in the morning, working through his private boxes which contained the information that had come in overnight, already arranged in order of importance by the team of private secretaries he gathered around him. One of his three typists, using a specially designed silent typewriter, or his short-hand writer, would take down the various minutes and notes he dictated before he actually got out of bed. After finally getting up, he would attend to whatever business was required, attending committee meetings and the like, but making sure to have a break for lunch, often accompanied by champagne and followed by brandy.

A map room was set up in the Admiralty so that he could keep track of the fleet, and he would spend hours studying it, often until the early hours of the morning. His old friend Brendan Bracken was appointed his Parliamentary Private Secretary, and Professor Frederick Lindemann, another old friend, became his chief scientific advisor and the head of his newly created statistical office, which collated the enormous amount of information obtained by Churchill into short and succinct reports so that he had easily at hand all the relevant information on whichever subject he required.

In the first few months of the war the threat from U-boats in the Western Approaches of the North Atlantic resulted in the sinking of a number of naval and merchant ships. Churchill initiated plans for all merchant ships to travel in escorted convoys and for all naval ships to be fitted with ASDIC equipment, as the British submarine detecting sonar system was known. The most serious loss was the *Royal Oak*, a battleship which was attacked and sunk while at anchor in Scapa Flow on 14 October by a U-boat which had penetrated the submarine defences. More than 800 of the 1,200 crew were lost. In December, the first naval engagement of the war, the Battle of the River Plate, was fought off the coast of Argentina and Uruguay. Although the Royal Navy suffered more losses in the battle, it was considered a British victory because the German pocket battleship *Graf Spee* was damaged and had to be scuttled a few days later.

One of Churchill's main concerns while he was at the Admiralty was to develop plans for offensive action, both to take the war to the Germans and to raise morale at home. As ever, he did not confine his thinking to naval operations alone and, since he was now a member of the War Cabinet, he had more scope to plan for other fields of operation than during the previous war. Not all of his plans were well thought out, particularly the idea of sending a naval squadron into the Baltic where it would have been highly vulnerable to attack from German aircraft if the plan had gone ahead. But he was keen to develop other ideas for operations in Scandinavia, principally in an effort to stop the transport of iron ore from mines in Sweden to Germany through the northern Norwegian port of Narvik. The ore was an essential resource for German industry so, if a way could be found to prevent it from getting to Germany, the whole of the German war effort could be brought to a halt. The tactics can be seen as part of the overall British strategy of playing for time, avoiding direct confrontations on the Western Front while the military capability of the country was built up over a period of several years.

From November onwards, Churchill devised a number of different plans to stop the ore reaching Germany. These included laying mines along the Norwegian coast to force transport ships out into international waters, where they could legitimately be attacked, and landing troops at Narvik which could then advance on the mines in Sweden. But, with both Norway and Sweden maintaining neutrality, the War Cabinet failed to make a decision on what to do and the Allied forces assembled to mount an operation remained in Britain. Towards the end of March 1940, a plan was finally agreed but, on 9 April, before it could be put into effect, Germany invaded both Norway and Denmark.

The Allied operation went ahead, with troops landing near the now-occupied Narvik and at Trondheim in central Norway, but the initiative which might have been gained by launching the operation earlier, as Churchill had wanted, had been lost. By the end of April the Allied forces were withdrawn from Trondheim and, even though they remained in position around Narvik until June, it was apparent that the Norway Campaign was heading for failure. This prompted a debate in the House of Commons, the result of which would have far-reaching implications for the British Government and its conduct of the rest of the war.

The Finest Hours

The Norway Debate began on 7 May with Chamberlain explaining why the withdrawal from Trondheim had been necessary. It quickly expanded from its original scope, as MPs from all sides of the House began to criticise the Government for its handling of the war. The speeches made from the Conservative benches were particularly damaging to Chamberlain. Sir Roger Keyes, an Admiral of the Fleet as well as an MP, was scathing about the conduct of the war, and his argument was given extra force because he was assumed to have inside knowledge as a consequence of the position he held. The prominent Conservative backbench MP Leo Amery, speaking to Chamberlain directly, quoted the words Oliver Cromwell had said in 1653 when he forcibly evicted the Long Parliament, 'You have sat too long here for any good you have been doing. Depart, I say, and let us have done with you. In the name of God, go'.

On the second day of the debate, Churchill robustly defended the conduct of the Government during the campaign, even though, in private, he had been extremely critical of the numerous delays. At the end of the debate a vote was held on a Motion of Censure of the Government's conduct, which, although not a Vote of No Confidence, effectively amounted to the same thing. Many Conservative MPs voted against the Government which won the motion but with a much reduced majority.

It was a devastating blow for Chamberlain and a direct challenge to his leadership. With his position apparently untenable, he decided that the only way forward was to form a coalition National Government by inviting the opposition Labour Party to join with the Conservatives and Liberals. Clement Atlee, the Leader of the Opposition, refused the offer, saying that Labour would not serve in a Government with Chamberlain as Prime Minister. On 9 May, Chamberlain asked Lord Halifax, the Foreign Secretary, and Churchill, together with the Conservative Chief Whip David Margesson, to a meeting to discuss the situation and to decide on a successor if he was to resign. Prior to the meeting, Churchill had been advised that, when the question of leadership was raised, he should keep quiet and allow Halifax, Chamberlain's preferred choice, to speak first. When the moment came Churchill followed the advice and waited for what, he would later write, felt like several minutes. Halifax finally spoke, saying that his position in the House of Lords would make it difficult for him to be an effective leader and that he thought that Churchill would be a better choice.

The following morning brought the news that German forces had begun to invade Belgium, Holland and France, bringing the Phoney War to an abrupt and shattering end. Hitler had unleashed the *blitzkrieg*, sending heavily-armoured and mobile units of his army, supported by overwhelming air power, to smash through the relatively lightly-defended region of the Ardennes and into central Belgium. It was a critical moment in the war and, at first, Chamberlain thought of staying on as Prime Minister while the crisis lasted. But, during the day, he was persuaded to step down, going to Buckingham Palace that evening to tender his resignation to the King. Going against protocol, he recommended that the King send for Churchill to form the next administration.

Later that evening, Churchill was summoned to the palace and invited to form a Government. He accepted, fulfilling an ambition he had held for forty years. At the age of sixty-five, at a time when he had been written off as a politician on numerous occasions, he had finally become Prime Minister at one of the most momentous times in the entire history of Britain. He immediately invited Atlee to join a coalition and began to put together his Government, working well into the night. After the war he wrote in his memoirs:

> As I went to bed that night at about 3am, I was conscious of a profound sense of relief. At last I had the authority to give directions over the whole scene. I felt as if I was walking with destiny, and that all my past life had been but a preparation for this hour and for this trial.

The following morning he began the task of reorganising the Government to address the problems he had earlier perceived in its inability to reach decisions and take affirmative action quickly. This process would continue for several months against the backdrop of the worsening situation of the war but it would also be essential for Britain's future that the resulting structure was efficient and fit for the purpose.

The War Cabinet was reconstituted with five members, and Attlee and Arthur Greenwood from the Labour Party joined Churchill, Chamberlain and Halifax. The personnel changed a number of times thereafter, with Chamberlain retiring through ill health in September and Halifax being given the job of British Ambassador to America in January 1941, but the basic structure remained the same.

Churchill also created a new position of Minister of Defence, which he took himself. This allowed him to remain in close contact with the Chiefs of Staff of the three services, with General Hastings Ismay acting as a liaison between the Chiefs of Staff Committee and the War Cabinet, and Churchill meeting almost daily with both. As with the War Cabinet, the personnel changed during the war but, once it became apparent that the new structure worked, it remained in place. It solved the problem that had arisen in the First World War of a split between the politicians and the military and, as the war went on, major decisions were still taken by the War Cabinet but Churchill and the Chiefs of Staff were increasingly allowed to get on with the conduct of the war without undue interference.

One of the strengths of Churchill's Government was that it was not dictatorial. This was in great contrast to the German administration, in which Hitler was not challenged by his subordinates for fear of the repercussions. Churchill encouraged people to speak their minds and would often refine plans through a process of debate which could, on occasion, dissolve into blazing rows. But, whether he agreed with it or not, Churchill respected the final decision, reached by majority vote even when, as regularly happened, it went against him.

Three days after Churchill became Prime Minister, German panzers broke through the French defences at a weak point in the line near the town of Sedan and advanced rapidly into France, threatening to split the Allied forces. On the same day, 13 May, Churchill made his first speech as Prime Minister, saying, 'I have nothing to offer but blood, toil, tears and sweat'. He then spelt out what his war objectives were:

> You ask, what is our aim? I can answer in one word: Victory. Victory at all costs. Victory in spite of all terror. Victory, however long and hard the road may be, for without victory there is no survival.

Given the circumstances, it was a brave statement and it was the first of a series of speeches he made to the House over the next few months, some of which were later broadcast on the radio, aimed at fortifying the British people against the hardships that were to come. The boost to morale these speeches provided would prove to be one of Churchill's greatest contributions towards winning the war, and some of the resonant phrases he used are now amongst the most recognisable words in the English language.

The dire consequences of a loss of morale were made plain to Churchill over the next few weeks during the trips he made to France to discuss the worsening situation and to attempt to instil some fighting spirit in those French leaders and generals who were wavering in their enthusiasm to continue the war. On one occasion General Gamelin, the commander of the French Army until he was replaced by General Weygand, gave details of the rapid German advance. Churchill asked him where the French reserves were located, to which the general replied with a single word, 'Aucune', meaning, 'There are none'. Churchill would later say that this was the biggest shock he had received throughout the entire war as it meant that there was no means of stopping the German advance.

The French made repeated requests for more help from Britain, asking particularly that more squadrons of fighter planes should be sent over. But, with the situation becoming increasingly hopeless, Churchill, with the agreement of the Chiefs of Staff and War Cabinet, decided that such a move would weaken Britain's own defences too much. This would become a source of bitterness between Britain and France, as would the decision to withdraw the British Expeditionary Force from France through Dunkirk. Operation Dynamo, as it was called, began on 26 May, with 333,000 troops being brought back to Britain by 3 June, more than 100,000 of whom were French. Nonetheless a vast amount of equipment, including tanks and artillery that Britain could hardly afford to lose, had to be left behind.

While this operation was being carried out, the War Cabinet began to debate whether it was possible to continue the war at all in the light of the imminent fall of France. Mussolini had offered to mediate in negotiations between Britain and Germany to bring about a peaceful settlement and Halifax, with some support from Chamberlain, argued in favour of taking up the offer. Churchill was vehemently opposed to any sort of negotiations with 'that man', as he referred to Hitler, and was supported by Attlee and Greenwood. At a meeting of the full Cabinet, he forcefully expressed his view that any deal reached with Germany would lead to Britain becoming a Nazi puppet state. He went on to say, ' If this long island story of ours is to end at last, let it end only when each one of us is choking in his own blood upon the ground'. His words were greeted by cheers from all, including Chamberlain, meaning that Churchill had persuaded everybody in Government to fight on to the end no matter what. A few weeks later he issued a general instruction to all Government ministers that they should not make any defeatist comments in public at any time, no matter what they thought in private.

Even at this dark time, there were a few rays of light, including the success of British code-breakers based at Bletchley Park in Buckinghamshire in deciphering intercepted German radio communications sent by their Enigma encryption machines. It had come too late to warn of the invasion of France, which had caught the Allies completely by surprise, but had been extremely useful during the evacuation of troops from Dunkirk. Ultra, as the intelligence information from this source was known, would prove vital to the Allies throughout the course of the war and Churchill, who was well aware of the importance of intelligence, made strenuous efforts to ensure that it remained secret. Less than thirty people outside Bletchley were aware of the source of the intelligence.[10]

In a speech to the House of Commons, later broadcast, Churchill pulled no punches, saying:

Even though large parts of Europe and many old and famous States have fallen or may fall into the grip of the Gestapo and all the odious apparatus of Nazi rule, we shall not flag or fail. We shall go on to the end, we shall fight in France, we shall fight on the seas and oceans, we shall fight with growing confidence and growing strength in the air, we shall defend our Island, whatever the cost may be, we shall fight on the beaches, we shall fight on the landing grounds, we shall fight in the fields and in the streets, we shall fight in the hills; we shall never surrender, and even if, which I do not for a moment believe, this Island or a large part of it were subjugated and starving, then our Empire beyond the seas, armed and guarded by the British Fleet, would carry on the struggle, until, in God's good time, the New World, with all its power and might, steps forth to the rescue and the liberation of the Old.

The reference to the New World was, of course, aimed at America. Churchill had been in regular contact by telegram with President Franklin D. Roosevelt since October 1939 and, although he was aware that the political situation in America would prevent Roosevelt from joining the Allies in the immediate future, he was confident that America would come in after the Presidential elections in November. In the meantime, Roosevelt offered as much support as he could, supplying Britain with vast amounts of food and military equipment despite America's declared position as a non-belligerent. This was initially paid for in cash, with Britain shipping gold to America, but when the gold reserves began to run low in early 1941, a system of credit known as lend-lease was devised,[11] together with a deal by which fifty American destroyers were sent to Britain in exchange for leases on military bases, mostly located on British possessions around the Caribbean.

However, Churchill was well aware in June 1941 that Britain would have to fight on alone for the foreseeable future. Bad news kept coming. Italy declared war on Britain and France on 10 June, opening up a theatre of war around the Mediterranean, and German troops entered Paris three days later. On 18 June, Churchill made his third great speech to the House of Commons, saying, 'What General Weygand has called the Battle of France is over. I suspect that the Battle of Britain is about to begin.' He continued:

> Hitler knows that he will have to break us in this Island or lose the war. If we can stand up to him, all Europe may be freed and the life of the world may move forward into broad, sunlit uplands. But if we fail, then the whole world, including the United States, including all that we have known and cared for, will sink into the abyss of a new Dark Age made more sinister, and perhaps more protracted, by the lights of perverted science. Let us therefore brace ourselves to our duties, and so bear ourselves, that if the British Empire and its Commonwealth last for a thousand years, men will still say, "This was their finest hour."

In private Churchill could be less eloquent, often adding the phrase 'KBO' to whatever he was saying, the letters standing for 'Keep Buggering On'.

Four days after the 18 June speech, France signed an armistice with Germany, and the country was nominally divided between Occupied France and the area governed by Vichy France under the leadership of the ageing Marshal Pétain, the hero of Verdun in the First World War. (In 1945, Pétain would be tried and found guilty of treason by a French court.) One of the German conditions in the armistice was for the surrender of the French Fleet, much of which was stationed at the naval base of Mers-el-Kebir near the city of Oran in Algeria. Churchill, together with the rest of the War Cabinet, was not prepared to allow these ships to fall into German hands and, after the French commanding officer refused to comply with a British ultimatum to that effect, Royal Naval ships opened fire, putting most of the French ships out of action and killing almost 1,300 French sailors. It was a ruthless and cold-blooded attack on the armed forces of a country which had been an ally only weeks beforehand, and it sent a very clear message to the rest of the world that Britain was going to fight on no matter what it took.

Ultra intelligence and aerial reconnaissance both confirmed the build up of German troops and equipment on the other side of the channel and, with the threat of invasion imminent, much of Britain's war effort was directed into defensive measures across a huge swath of southern and eastern England. Churchill had already instigated the formation of the Home Guard, a body of men mostly too old to join the regular army. In order to ensure that measures were being taken to take the war to Germany, he also issued instructions to set up Commando units to carry out raids across the channel and the Special Operations Executive (SOE) to develop espionage and sabotage behind enemy lines. He regularly toured the defence preparations, which were commanded by General Alan Brooke (later Lord Alanbrooke), who would go on to succeed General Sir John Dill as the Chief of the Imperial General Staff and become one of the main architects of the war.

Throughout July, German air raids intensified, mainly targeting industrial areas and docklands. From 10 July, squadrons of German fighter planes began to sweep across Britain in an attempt to break the RAF, and airfields and aeroplane factories became the main target for bombers. The Battle of Britain, as Churchill had called it, had begun in earnest. For Operation Sealion, the German plan for the invasion of Britain, to have a reasonable chance of success, Germany needed to achieve air supremacy over the English Channel and the south of England. The Royal Navy far exceeded the *Kriegsmarine*, the

German Navy, so, without air supremacy, German shipping carrying an invading force across the channel would be highly vulnerable.

At the same time as the war in the air was developing, the Battle of the Atlantic intensified, as German surface raiders and U-boats sank an increasing tonnage of merchant vessels transporting supplies to Britain. As well as tying up Royal Naval vessels in the North Atlantic, keeping them away from the English Channel, the Germans were attempting to sever Britain's lifeline and strangle the country into submission.

As the Luftwaffe continued the onslaught, with day and night bombing raids and dogfights between fighter planes in the skies over the South of England, their losses began to mount up. Although they had numerical supremacy over the RAF, they could only remain over England for a maximum of 30 minutes before they had to return to their bases in occupied Europe to refuel. RAF pilots were fighting almost over the top of their airfields, giving them an advantage which went a long way towards nullifying the greater number of German planes.

On 16 August, Churchill visited the headquarters of 11 Group Fighter Command in Uxbridge, sitting in the gallery around the operations room to watch as the positions of wave after wave of German planes crossing the channel were marked on the map table below. At one point in the day, every squadron in the group was in the air at the same time. After he had left, Churchill said to General Ismay, in words he would later use in a speech, 'Never in the field of human conflict has so much been owed by so many to so few'. With its echoes of the St Crispin's Day speech in Shakespeare's *Henry V*, when the King rouses his army on the eve of the Battle of Agincourt, in which the English defeated a much larger French army,[12] it became, perhaps, his most memorable phrase, and the pilots who flew in the Battle of Britain became known as 'the Few',

The Luftwaffe maintained the pressure for a further month, with day and night bombing raids directed against British air defences. The attritional rate on pilots and planes was high on both sides, but Germany lost decisively more and, since they were fighting over enemy territory, they recovered fewer of those pilots who had been shot down. Churchill claimed that the ratio of planes shot down was three to one in favour of Britain which, like many statistics made public during the war, was an exaggeration. The actual rate was nearer to two to one but, whatever the truth of the matter, it was becoming clear by September that the RAF was winning and that, for the first time since the start of the war, German armed forces had been beaten.

Intelligence reports suggested that, if an invasion was going to come, it would be in those first few weeks of September and there were a number of false alarms suggesting that the Germans were coming. After the war, captured documents made clear that Hitler had set a date of 15 September for the invasion, a day that saw some of the most intense aerial battles and would later become known as Battle of Britain Day. But those same documents also showed that, by then, the invasion had been postponed because of Germany's inability to gain air supremacy. Some military historians have since suggested that Hitler never actually intended to invade Britain but was only threatening to do so in an attempt to draw Britain to the nego-tiating table and to distract attention away from his other plans. If that was the case, then he went to extraordinary lengths to make the deception convincing. Amongst other preparations, over 200 self-propelled barges were assembled in the ports of

France and the Low Countries in readiness to carry the invading army.

During the first week of September, German raids began to switch from targeting air defences to bombing cities, beginning what would quickly become known as the Blitz. From 7 September onwards, London was bombed on 57 consecutive nights, and Manchester, Birmingham, Cardiff and Belfast were among many other cities to be raided. On 14 November, Coventry was bombed with a combination of high explosive and incendiary bombs which destroyed much of the centre of the city, killing more than 500 civilians and leaving the cathedral in ruins. Churchill visited the scene some time later to see the damage for himself. Throughout the months of the Blitz, in order to be seen by the people, he travelled to the scenes of the worst bombing. On a number of occasions during these visits he was moved to tears by the extraordinary resilience shown by people who had been bombed out of their houses, many of whom exhorted him to take the fight back to Hitler.

While London was being subjected to such regular bombing raids, Churchill used the underground Central War Rooms in Whitehall, later known as the Cabinet War Rooms[13], in order to continue conducting the business of Government without having to move out of the city. Churchill's safety was a constant concern throughout the war. The same bodyguard he had been assigned while a Government minister in the 1920s, Detective Inspector Walter H. Thompson, accompanied him wherever he went, with Churchill often travelling under the alias of Colonel Warden.

Churchill's health was another major concern. He was in his late sixties and had smoked and drunk prodigiously for much of his life, to the extent that anybody emulating him these days would surely be regarded as an alcoholic. Such private indulgences, together with the incredible stress of the responsibilities he carried, must have impacted on his health and were probably the causes of the periods of exhaustion and depression he experienced, which could occasionally manifest themselves as petulant and boorish behaviour. On one occasion in June 1940, Clementine Churchill, perhaps the only person who could raise the subject, wrote to him to ask him to stop being overbearing and sarcastic towards his staff, knowing that he was more likely to pay attention to the written word than if she had spoken to him on the subject.

Ensuring that Churchill had sufficient rest became of paramount importance as the war dragged on. His personal doctor Charles Wilson (later Lord Moran), prescribed sleeping pills as well as medicines for Churchill's frequent illnesses and gave him regular health checks. Chartwell had been closed up for the duration of the war because it was considered to be too close to the English Channel to be safe, so Churchill made frequent use of Chequers in Buckinghamshire, the official country residence of the Prime Minister, as a weekend retreat. With the location of the official residence being so well known, including to the Germans, he also spent some weekends at the more secluded country house of Ditchley in Oxfordshire, particularly those which coincided with a full moon, when the long winding drive leading to Chequers would have made the house easily identifiable from the air.

But even though weekends at Chequers and Ditchley were more restful than his working week, the war didn't take a break for the weekend and Churchill continued to send minutes and work at his boxes from wherever he was. Most weekends in the country included the presence of various eminent people and members of Churchill's personal staff, who had been invited to dinner or to stay for the weekend. Some of the most important figures in the war effort would often find themselves discussing the direction of the war with Churchill over a whiskey and soda and then having dinner with whichever members of his family were also there. One of Churchill's favourite after-dinner activities at Chequers was to watch films and, on one occasion on 10 May 1941, when he was told after dinner that Hitler's deputy Rudolf Hess had been captured in Scotland, he is reported to have said, 'Hess or no Hess, I'm going to watch the Marx Brothers'.

The punishing travel schedule Churchill maintained throughout the war also had implications for the state of his health, and Dr Wilson became a regular member of his entourage, together with Detective Inspector Thompson and his various advisers and private secretaries. During his first visit to Washington in December 1941, Churchill suffered a mild heart attack and was treated by Wilson. But rather than taking some time off, as Wilson advised, he continued with most of his engagements in order to hide the nature of his illness, which remained secret for the duration of the war.

The End of the Beginning

The Battle of Britain may have been won, but British forces suffered a series of disastrous reverses afterwards which dented even Churchill's formidable confidence. The North African campaign was progressing reasonably well until the Italian forces there were reinforced in February 1941 by the Africa Korps under the command of Erwin Rommel. The two armies fought backwards and forwards across the Western Desert throughout much of 1941 and 1942. Benghazi, for instance, the second largest city in Libya, changed hands on no less than five occasions.

Greece fell to the invading German army in April 1941, and the 50,000 British and Commonwealth troops Churchill had sent to the country to aid the Greek army were forced into a rapid evacuation. Crete suffered a similar fate in the following month. It was subjected to an initial attack by German airborne troops which, despite losses so heavy Hitler did not attempt anything similar again, managed to establish themselves against a large defending force so that German reinforcements could be sent in by plane. Perhaps the only shred of good news was Hitler's attack on Russia in June 1941, which was initially carried out with devastating effect but which meant that the Russians were now fighting on the same side as Britain.

The situation in the Far East towards the end of 1941 was hardly any better. In an early draft of his war memoirs Churchill wrote that he had danced at the news of the Japanese attack on Pearl Harbour, knowing that America would now be entering the war. He edited out these comments for the published edition, knowing the offence they would cause in America which had suffered the loss of almost 2,500 men in the attack. But there was nothing to dance about in the immediate aftermath of Pearl Harbour, with almost simultaneous and successful Japanese assaults being launched against the Philippines, Malaya and Hong Kong. The two warships Britain had belatedly sent to the Far East, the battlecruiser *Repulse* and the battleship *Prince of Wales*, were both sunk off Singapore two days after Pearl Harbour by Japanese torpedo planes, which meant that the Royal Navy could do little about the invasion of Malaya. Thailand also capitulated immediately and allied itself with Japan, leaving the way open for the invasion of Burma. This followed in January 1942 and threatened to take the war into India.

Churchill came under increasing pressure in the House of Commons after this series of setbacks and he demanded a Vote of Confidence debate as the Japanese were advancing down the Malay Peninsula towards Singapore. The vote came out overwhelmingly in his favour, with the only vote against him coming from a left-wing and slightly eccentric independent MP. But in his speech in the debate Churchill, who had been made aware of the inadequacy of the defences of Singapore only shortly beforehand, warned there would be 'worse to come'. Few preparations had been taken to meet an attack from the landward side of Singapore Island, the direction from which the Japanese forces were now approaching, and the bulk of the defensive measures had been directed towards repelling a seaborne invasion. Despite the garrison on Singapore containing 130,000 men, more, Churchill estimated, than the entire Japanese force in Malaya, the British commander was forced to surrender an impossible situation on 15 February. It was the largest capitulation in British military history, and 80,000 troops, mainly from India, Australia and Britain, were taken into captivity. A significant number of them would join other Allied Prisoners of War as forced labour in the construction of the Burma Railway, from which many did not return.

It was certainly a low point in Churchill's war leadership and one for which he bore some of the responsibility, having consistently underestimated the threat Japanese forces posed to the Allies in the Far East. In his defence it could be argued that his attention had been fully engaged in Britain and North Africa during this period and that he had not been kept adequately informed by his senior commanders in the field. But, in an uncharacteristic admission of failure in his war memoirs, Churchill partially accepted the blame, saying that he might not have been told exactly what was occurring but he should have asked the relevant questions.

In the summer of 1942, Rommel launched an attack in the Western Desert which pushed the British back into Egypt, before he was stopped at the coastal town of El Alamein, about 65 miles west of Alexandria. Churchill and Brooke flew to Cairo in August to assess the situation for themselves and to go on a morale-boosting tour of the British forces in the desert. In his usual manner Churchill had been badgering General Claude Auchinleck, the commander of the British forces, to go on the offensive. During the visit, and with Brooke's agreement, he decided to replace Auchinleck with General Harold Alexander, one of his favourite generals, who had previously commanded the evacuation of Dunkirk as well as the successful fighting retreat of the Allied forces from Burma into India.

Churchill was also instrumental in the appointment of General Bernard Montgomery to commander of the Eighth Army, thus setting in place the senior commanders for a counter-offensive against Rommel. He had initially favoured General William Gott for the post but Gott was killed when the plane he was travelling in was shot down on the way from the El Alamein to Cairo, a journey Churchill himself had taken a few days previously. On approving Montgomery's appointment after Gott's death, Churchill is said to have remarked that he hoped that Montgomery's famously abrasive character would be as unpleasant for the enemy as it was for his colleagues.

The offensive, the Second Battle of El Alamein, came

towards the end of October. It was timed to occur a few weeks before Operation Torch, the combined British and American operation commanded by General Dwight D. Eisenhower in which landings were made on the Atlantic coast of Morocco and the Mediterranean coast of Tunisia. The success at Alamein, the only land battle won by British forces on their own during the war, was helped to a great extent by Ultra intelligence which revealed Rommel's tactics and that his forces were rapidly running out of supplies and fuel. And Montgomery may have been a difficult personality but there is no doubt that both his tactics and the way in which he inspired the men of the Eighth Army under his command played a crucial role in the victory. The German forces were not only being pushed back out of Egypt but right through Libya and into Tunisia as well. It proved to be the crucial turning point in the North African Campaign and, when Churchill was confident of success, he said in a speech:

> The Germans have received back again that measure of fire and steel which they have so often meted out to others. Now this is not the end. It is not even the beginning of the end. But it is, perhaps, the end of the beginning.

While the British and American forces were pushing the Germans back in the desert, the German army had advanced into southern Russia with the intention of capturing the oil fields of Central Asia. They were stopped by the Red Army at Stalingrad and became engaged in one of the bloodiest and most brutal battles ever fought. By February 1943, an entire German army had been destroyed in what really was the beginning of the end for Nazi Germany.

Churchill, Roosevelt and Stalin

After Russia and America entered the war in 1941, Churchill may have rejoiced in the knowledge that the Allies would eventually win. However, the way in which victory was to be achieved relied on the co-operation of the three major Allied participants who did not necessarily agree on strategy and certainly differed in their ultimate war aims. Communication between the Big Three, as Churchill, Roosevelt and Stalin came to be called, occurred regularly but Churchill was well aware of the benefits to be gained from face-to-face meetings in which problems could be ironed out and decisions taken. In this spirit he travelled extensively, particularly in 1943, to attend conferences, clocking up more than 100,000 miles in the process.

At the heart of this diplomatic effort was Churchill's relationship with Roosevelt. As early as the summer of 1940, they had agreed that Britain and America should share scientific information which effectively meant Britain giving America its research on radar, the jet engine and atomic weaponry. The first of the nine meetings between the two men would have occurred in August 1941, four months before America entered the war, on board HMS *Prince of Wales*, the battleship later sunk off Malaya, then at a secure anchorage in a Newfoundland harbour. The outcome of this meeting was the Atlantic Charter, an initial agreement on aims for the post-war period and, as such, the basis for numerous international treaties signed after the war. Although neither side broached the subject directly, the different aims of Britain and America beyond the defeat of the Axis powers became increasingly apparent. In a nutshell, Britain was fighting to defend the old world order, in which it had been a world leader, while America was seeking to create a new world based on its own economic and military power. America ultimately achieved its aim, partially at the expense of Britain, which has led some historians to point to the Newfoundland meeting as the moment when a shift in world power occurred.

Churchill travelled to America twice in 1942 to hold conferences with Roosevelt in Washington. These were primarily concerned with war strategy and resulted in the 'Germany first' policy in which America agreed to divert most of its resources towards fighting the greater enemy in Europe before turning its attention to Japan. But serious differences soon emerged over how victory in Europe could be achieved. Put simply, America was too eager for military action and Britain too cautious. Churchill, as he had done in the First World War, was constantly coming up with plans to take the war to Germany and Italy in areas other than in Western Europe, and he was particularly keen on operations in various parts of the Mediterranean. These were mostly seen as peripheral by the Americans, sideshows to the main event which was the invasion of France.

At the conference held in Casablanca in 1943, Roosevelt agreed to one of Churchill's Mediterranean plans, perhaps the last time the Americans allowed themselves to be led by the British. Churchill wanted the British and American forces in North Africa to cross the Mediterranean and invade Sicily and then continue on to the Italian mainland. This would mean delaying any possible operations in France until 1944. The Casablanca Conference was also notable for the declaration made by the Allies that, unlike in the First World War which ended by means of an armistice and a negotiated peace settlement, they would prosecute the war until they had achieved the unconditional surrender of Germany. In addition, Churchill engineered a meeting between the two French generals, de Gaulle and Giraud, who were vigorously opposing each other for the overall leadership of the Free French forces. Churchill had previously remarked in private that he thought the French fought each other more intensely than they fought the Germans and, in a famous photograph from Casablanca in which de Gaulle and Giraud are shown shaking hands, he is sitting down next to them with what can only be described as a smirk on his face.

The Big Three met together for the first time at the Tehran Conference, held over three days towards the end of November 1943. Churchill had met Stalin once before, in Moscow in August 1942, and had established a cordial working relationship but the extent of the co-operation between the two is much harder to gauge than that between Churchill and Roosevelt. The impression given is that Churchill never really knew Stalin's real intentions and that, to some extent, he was prepared to take the Soviet leader's words at face value. At later meetings, in Yalta in 1945 and Potsdam in 1946, both concerned with the shape of the post-war world, Churchill accepted Stalin's word that Russia was prepared to allow the countries of Eastern Europe to form democratic institutions when, as would quickly become apparent, Stalin had no intention of doing so.

Roosevelt met Stalin in private on a number of occasions in Tehran, giving Churchill an indication that he was being sidelined. It was becoming apparent who the major powers were, and Churchill was forced to admit, in his own words, 'what a small nation we are'. For some time Stalin had wanted the Allies to open a second front against Germany in the west to take some of the pressure off the Red Army in the east and, in Tehran, he got what he wanted – a commitment from Britain and America to begin Operation Overlord, the invasion of France, in the following year.

Overlord

One of the reasons the British Chiefs of Staff were reluctant to commit themselves to Overlord was that they had reached the conclusion that the German army, on a man-to-man basis, was superior to those of both Britain and America. If battles were fought in which the opposing forces were equal, they concluded that the Germans would most likely win, so they advocated the use of overwhelming force to guarantee victory. Such thinking may have been behind Churchill's continued support for operations in the Mediterranean and in other parts of Europe. Rather than a frontal assault against the German forces in France, which had been so costly in the First World War, he wanted to attack what he described as the 'soft under-belly' of Italy first.

Another tactic to take the war to the enemy without great armies engaging in France was the strategic area bombing of German cities. Arthur 'Bomber' Harris, the head of Bomber Command, together with Professor Lindemann, had convinced Churchill by February 1942 that Germany could be defeated by a concerted campaign of area bombing of cities. Despite the questionable morality of this strategy, it was adopted ahead of the precision bombing of military and industrial targets which could only be accurately achieved in daylight when the bombers involved were most vulnerable to attack. It was controversial at the time (and remains so today) but it was widely supported by the public and authorised by Churchill who bore the ultimate responsibility.

Churchill may not have been overly enthusiastic about Overlord but, by committing Britain to achieving the unconditional surrender of Germany at the Casablanca Conference, he was accepting that the air war would not defeat Germany on its own and that a land war across Western Europe was inevitable. However, before Overlord was launched, he wanted to go ahead with the invasion of Italy which he hoped would deflect German forces away from France and open up a front against Germany as troops advanced through Italy and into Austria. It was the beginning of his overall plan to advance into Central Europe and extend the war into Greece and the Balkans. Few senior commanders thought the overall plan was feasible, regarding it as one of Churchill's 'midnight follies', grand schemes which came to him in flashes of inspiration and which he had to be dissuaded from pursuing, usually by Alan Brooke.

The Italian campaign began with the invasion of Sicily in July 1943 which succeeded in capturing the island in six weeks. The subsequent landings at Salerno on the Italian mainland in early September precipitated the Italian Government (no longer headed by Mussolini who had been overthrown) into seeking an immediate armistice. Churchill had expected Hitler to abandon Italy at this point but, rather than doing so, the Führer sent German forces to occupy the country and to form a strong defensive line south of Rome in order to prevent the Allies from advancing up the peninsula. Intense fighting developed, particularly around the mountain stronghold of Monte Cassino, and, in an attempt to outflank the German defences, the Anzio landings of January 1944 took place. Churchill strongly favoured this operation, which was ultimately intended to allow the Allies to capture Rome, and was highly critical of its commanders when it bogged down. He believed them to have been too cautious, saying, 'I had hoped at Anzio to land a wildcat. Instead I have beached a whale'.

In the event Rome was not finally captured until 4 June, the day before Overlord was due to be launched and the Italian campaign continued until the eventual German surrender in May 1945. It put an end to Churchill's ideas of attacking Germany through the 'underbelly' of Europe. But with air supremacy being achieved over France, the Battle of the Atlantic at a stage where the German Navy could not oppose an Allied invasion force from crossing the channel, and a huge force of American soldiers and arms having been built up in Britain, nothing now stood in the way of Overlord.

Churchill had agreed to Roosevelt's request for an American to be in command of Overlord, even though he had previously promised the job to Brooke. With the British army already approaching its maximum capacity, it was apparent that the bulk of the forces used would have to be American. Eisenhower was given the job, even though he was not considered a battlefield general and didn't actually have any frontline experience. It proved to be the right choice. Ike, as he was usually called, was a brilliant administrator and politician which he needed to be in order to deal with the large and often difficult personalities involved – not only Churchill himself but also Montgomery and the American generals Omar Bradley and George S. Patton.

Montgomery was given command of the land forces, putting him in charge of much of the planning for the largest amphibious landings ever attempted. As well as the plans for actually getting the Allied forces onto the beaches of

Normandy, a huge deception, known as Operation Fortitude, was devised to fool the Germans into thinking the invasion would occur in the Pas-de-Calais region of Northern France. Dummy divisions were created in East Anglia, together with the accompanying radio traffic, and fictitious reports from turned Nazi agents in Britain were compiled and sent to Germany. Patton was put in charge of these non-existent forces, after he had been temporarily relieved of his command following an incident in a hospital in which he had slapped an injured soldier. He made himself highly visible, on one occasion shortly before D-Day shouting to Eisenhower across a packed room in a London Hotel, 'See you in Calais'.

Eisenhower had selected 5 June as D-Day but poor weather conditions in the channel forced a postponement. With everything ready to go and the next occasion when the tides would be in favour of the landings a month away, he took the decision to go on the following day. The attack began with airborne troops being parachuted into the Normandy countryside and more special forces arriving by glider. They were intended to seize strategic bridges and generally to create chaos for the Germans. In most cases, the objectives were achieved but some of the parachute drops were in the wrong place. Units were widely scattered and some of the gliders crashed on landing. Before dawn, an intensive naval and aerial bombardment of the German defences of the Atlantic Wall in Normandy began and then, at 6.30 in the morning, H-Hour of D-Day, the first troops landed on the beaches.

The Americans went first, landing on the western sectors of the designated beaches known as Utah and Omaha, followed by the British and Canadians at Gold, Juno and Sword. The deception plans proved to have been highly effective and the landings took the defending forces completely by surprise. Even after the invasion had begun, some German commanders continued to believe it was a diversionary attack and that the real invasion would follow near Calais. The German response was also hampered by the absence of a number of senior officers who had taken leave in the belief that the rough weather in the channel would prevent an invasion. Rommel himself, the Commander-in-Chief of the German defences, had gone to Germany for a few days to spend time with his family.

Nonetheless, despite the slow German response to the landings, resistance was fierce in some of the sectors. This was particularly the case on Omaha beach, where the Americans took heavy casualties but nevertheless managed to overcome the defences and establish themselves inland. Few of the actual objectives, which had been deliberately made ambitious by Montgomery, were met on D-Day but a beachhead was formed over the next few days so that large numbers of troops and equipment could be shipped over. And casualties were less than had been expected, with about 3,000 men killed in total. True to form, Churchill, although he was 69 years old at the time, had wanted to cross the channel on D-Day to observe the landings himself. He was persuaded not to go by King George VI but nothing was going to stop him travelling across the channel a few days later. On 12 June, arriving on the beaches, he was met by Montgomery who took him on a tour of the beachhead.

By the time of Churchill's visit two artificial Mulberry harbours had been anchored into place and more than 300,000 men had come ashore but fierce fighting continued a few miles inland after the Germans had managed to organise their defence. It would take almost two months before British and Canadian forces took the city of Caen, one of the main strategic objectives. Monty was severely criticised by the Americans for the delay in taking the city. He was not a man who took criticism well, or readily admitted to his mistakes, and acrimonious disputes between him and Bradley and the reinstated Patton in particular continued for much of the rest of the campaign.

Montgomery's plan was for the British and Canadians to engage with the main German forces, allowing the American armies to be built up and then to lead the breakout from the beachhead. When the breakout came at the beginning of August, it was a spectacular success. The Americans under the command of Patton advanced rapidly into France, trapping most of the German forces that were west of the River Seine in what became known as the Falaise Pocket. It was the decisive moment in the Battle of Normandy and it opened up the way to Paris which was liberated on 25 August. There were many months of fierce fighting to come but the Allies were now on the road to Germany itself.

V for Victory

In the summer and autumn of 1944, the Allies were advancing towards Germany from the west, while, in the east, the Russians had begun a huge offensive in what is now Belarus and were pushing into Poland. It could only be a matter of time before Germany was defeated, but not everything went as well as the Allies had hoped. In September 1944, Operation Market Garden, the plan for airborne troops to seize the bridge over the Rhine at Arnhem in the Netherlands, was a failure and the Rhine, the last major obstacle to an advance into the German heartland, was not actually crossed until March of the following year. A huge German counter-offensive through the Ardennes, popularly known as the Battle of the Bulge, caught the Allies by surprise in December. It took them six weeks to contain and then push the Germans back, a feat achieved amidst even more bickering between Montgomery and the American generals.

A more serious, if less acrimonious, disagreement occurred between Eisenhower and Montgomery about the overall strategy of the Allied advance. Eisenhower favoured a 'broad front' policy, a relatively slow advance across a wide sector. Montgomery, supported by Churchill, preferred a much faster 'narrow front' advance which, although incurring greater risk, could potentially have allowed the Allies to reach Berlin and Prague before the Russians. By this time there were many more Americans involved in the fighting than British. Eisenhower decided to take overall command of the land battle in an effort to reduce the bickering between his senior commanders and so his strategy was the one that was adopted.

For much of this time, Churchill's attention was concentrated on what would happen in the countries which had been occupied by the Germans after the war was over. He continued his relentless schedule of travelling and, as he was repeatedly warned by Anthony Eden, the Foreign Minister, this was at the cost of ignoring domestic issues at home. In October 1944, he went to Moscow to meet Stalin, who was always rather paranoid about leaving Russia, to discuss the future of Greece and the Balkan countries. After some discussion, Churchill sketched out a rough plan on a single piece of paper detailing British and Russian spheres of interest, expressed as percentages. Britain, for example, was shown as being given a ninety percent interest in Greece and Russia a similar-sized interest in

Romania. Churchill passed the note over the table to Stalin who glanced at it and annotated the sketch with a large tick.

It was an unusual way of conducting diplomatic business but it appeared to work when the German withdrawal from Greece in December 1944 prompted a power struggle between the Greek Government and the Greek Communist Party and the country appeared to be heading for civil war. Churchill despatched British troops to Greece to support the Government and Stalin, apparently abiding by the agreement, refrained from sending any aid to the communists. But British troops fighting against Greeks who had resisted the German occupation, whether they were communists or not, did not go down well with the British press, not least when the battle for Europe was still raging.

Stalin's inaction over Greece was one of the reasons Churchill accepted his word over the future of Poland at the Yalta Conference, held over the first two weeks of February 1945. Stalin agreed to allow the Polish Government-in-Exile to return after the war in exchange for Russia keeping some Polish territory in the east of the country. It appears improbable that Stalin ever had any intention of keeping his word and it was naive of Churchill to expect him to do so, although when Soviet-backed communists took over Poland after the war, there was little he could have done about it short of starting another war.

After the Yalta Conference was over, Churchill remained in the Crimea for a period of rest and he was there when one of the most controversial Allied bombing raids of the war occurred. On the night of 14 February 1945, the centre of Dresden was almost completely destroyed by a combination of high explosive and incendiary bombs which caused an intense fire-storm to develop. The number of people killed is unknown and estimates vary widely, with the consensus view now suggesting that there were between 30,000 and 40,000 fatalities. At the time the raid was widely supported in Britain, although some dissenting voices questioned the necessity of bombing the city when it was apparent that the war was drawing to a close. After the war, and continuing today, the debate has broadened to question the morality of such tactics. The basic arguments revolve around the following question: to what extent is it justifiable to use methods which would be morally indefensible under any other circumstances to prosecute a war fought in a just cause?

Six weeks after the raid Churchill argued against continuing to bomb German cities and, after the war, he attempted to distance himself from the tactics of area bombing. But, even though it was the Deputy Prime Minister Clement Attlee who actually authorised the Dresden raid while Churchill was away and 'Bomber' Harris who was directly in command, there can be little doubt that Churchill, who had previously authorised Harris to bomb cities in the east of Germany, bore the ultimate responsibility. Dresden was specifically targeted due to a request from the Russians because the city was an important transportation centre for German troops going to the Eastern Front. Whether or not this constituted sufficient grounds for claiming that Dresden was a legitimate military target is open to question. The purpose of area bombing was, after all, to batter the German people into submission and, when we consider that the Allies were fighting a 'total war' against Hitler and Nazi Germany, a regime which committed the worst atrocities of genocide in history, it becomes easier to understand why such morally ambiguous tactics were used.

Not long after the bombing of Dresden, the Allies entered Germany and approached the Rhine. He had been persuaded to miss the D-Day landings but Churchill was not about to let the opportunity go by to observe what would be the last major Allied operation in Western Europe. He flew to the Netherlands on 23 March and was driven into Germany so that he could be with Montgomery the following morning to witness the beginning of the battle to cross the 400-yard-wide river near Wesel, a town which had by that time been completely flattened by aerial bombing and artillery fire.

The next day Churchill and Monty, accompanied by a small party of armed men, took a little trip across the river themselves, about ten miles away from the scene of the fighting. In his war memoirs, Churchill wrote, 'We landed in brilliant sunshine and perfect peace on the German shore, and walked about for half an hour or so unmolested'. After returning to the bank of the river held by the Allies, they travelled by car to within a few miles of the action in order to observe the Allied artillery and the German response. German shells began to burst in the river in front of their position and some went over their heads. An American general who was with them, worried about the danger from snipers as well as from the shelling, persuaded a reluctant Churchill, who seemed to be thoroughly enjoying himself, to move to a safer spot.

The zones of Allied control of an occupied Germany had already been agreed and, with Berlin in the Russian zone, Eisenhower decided to stop the advance into Germany and wait for the Red Army to take the German capital. Churchill wanted, as he put it, 'to shake hands with the Russians as far east as possible', but Roosevelt had already agreed this strategy with Stalin. There has been some suggestion that Roosevelt's rapidly-declining health towards the end of the war had impaired his judgement in this matter. The severity of his illness had been concealed from as many people as possible, including Churchill, and he died on 12 April from a cerebral haemor-rhage. Although a plane was made ready to take Churchill to Washington for the funeral, he inexplicably decided not to go, an uncharacteristic act by a man who put great store by the personal relationship he had developed with Roosevelt. His decision may have been a sign of the widening gap between the two leaders which opened towards the end of the war as Roosevelt effectively sidelined Churchill. Whatever his reason for not going, it deprived him of an early opportunity to meet Harry S. Truman, Roosevelt's successor as President.

On 30 April, with the Red Army fighting through the streets of Berlin, Hitler committed suicide. It was effectively the end of the war in Europe. Elements of the German Army attempted to break through the Russian forces surrounding Berlin so they could surrender to the British and Americans, delaying the final unconditional surrender until 7 May. Victory in Europe was celebrated the next day. Churchill appeared on the balcony of Buckingham Palace with the Royal Family and later addressed the huge crowd which had gathered in Whitehall from the balcony of the Ministry of Health. That night, before going to bed, he dealt with the pile of telegrams that had come in during the day, a routine he had kept up almost every day throughout the previous six years of war.

The Later Years

Defeat after Victory

Shortly after the defeat of Germany Churchill asked Clement Attlee, his deputy and the leader of the Labour Party, to continue with the Coalition Government until Japan was defeated. Attlee initially agreed, but he was not supported by the Labour Party as a whole. Although he was widely admired as a war leader, Churchill had alienated many of the other members of the coalition in the final few years of the war by appearing to favour the opinions of his circle of cronies, principally Lord Beaverbrook, Brendan Bracken and Professor Lindemann, over those of his Government ministers.

Two weeks after VE Day, Churchill resigned as Prime Minister and called a general election, although he continued in the role of caretaker Prime Minister[14] until the outcome of the election was known. He then made an ill-considered radio broadcast in which he suggested that any future Labour Government would behave in a totalitarian way, not tolerating any criticism and instituting 'some form of Gestapo' to ensure no other opinion than their own was heard. It was a gross insult to those members of the Labour Party who had served in the Government during the war and was a contributing factor to the Conservative Party's poor performance in the election when it was held in July. The

Labour Party won an overwhelming majority of seats in the House of Commons.

Churchill remained a hugely popular figure in Britain, and he was cheered everywhere he went, but he was also seen primarily as a war leader when what the British people wanted was to look forward towards a brighter future. During the war he had not paid any great attention to domestic policy in Britain, which had been mostly dealt with by Labour ministers in the coalition such as Ernest Bevin and Herbert Morrison. It allowed the Labour Party to become associated with the idea of post-war social reform and they based their election campaign on this, saying they would implement in full the findings of the Beveridge Report, which had been published in 1942 and had recommended the establishment of the Welfare State and the National Health Service.

The loss of the election came as a devastating blow to Churchill. It was described by Clementine as possibly being 'a blessing in disguise', to which Churchill replied that, if that was the case then, 'at the moment it seems quite effectively disguised'. However he felt about the loss, he certainly needed a rest and, in September, he left for a long holiday, staying near Lake Como in Italy and then moving on to the South of France.

Not only did Churchill gain the health benefits of the enforced rest but his reputation was not damaged in the difficult years of austerity immediately after the war finished, as Lloyd George's had been after the First World War. As the man who had foreseen the danger posed by Hitler, his opinion was widely respected on a diverse range of subjects and he was invited to speak at many different events, most famously in March 1946 at Westminster College in Fulton, Missouri. In the speech he referred to the danger posed to peace by the Soviet Union, saying:

From Stettin in the Baltic to Trieste in the Adriatic, an iron curtain has descended across the Continent. Behind that line lie all the capitals of the ancient states of Central and Eastern Europe. Warsaw, Berlin, Prague, Vienna, Budapest, Belgrade, Bucharest and Sofia, all these famous cities and the populations around them lie in what I must call the Soviet sphere, and all are subject in one form or another, not only to Soviet influence but to a very high and, in many cases, increasing measure of control from Moscow.

It was not the first time the term 'iron curtain' had been used but it was as a result of this speech that it entered common parlance to refer to the split between Western and Eastern Europe.

Churchill was also keen to promote co-operation between European states. He advocated the formation of the Council of Europe, although he would later refuse to join the European Coal and Steel Community, the forerunner of the European Union, when it was formed in 1951, seeing it as predominantly a French and German organisation. He was more interested in what he called the 'special relationship' between Britain and America, a term which remains in use today.

In 1946, shortly after returning to Britain from Fulton, Churchill began work on his war memoirs, assembling a team of researchers to help him, who became known as the Syndicate, and securing unprecedented permission to publish Government documents relating to the war, many of which he had originally written. The publishing deal he secured remains one of the largest ever signed, mainly because Churchill opted to be paid entirely in advance rather than by royalties accrued on sales and because the deal included serial rights in a number of newspapers and magazines. In America alone, the deal was worth $1.4 million and, for the first time in his life, he became a wealthy man.

Although he was still officially Leader of the Opposition, he spent much of his time at Chartwell writing *The Second World War*, a process which often involved him editing the work of the Syndicate and placing official documents in the text as much as it did dictating original material himself. He also continued to travel abroad regularly, staying in houses lent to him by wealthy friends and admirers and going on long cruises. This is not to say he didn't attend debates in the House of Commons, which he certainly did, but much of the day-to-day business of being in opposition was conducted by Anthony Eden who would have a long wait before officially becoming leader of the Conservative Party himself.

The Final Fling

A month before his 77th birthday Churchill returned to the office of Prime Minister after the Conservatives won the most seats at the general election held in October 1951. As well as inheriting the economic problems of post-war Britain, Churchill also had to deal with continuing problems in the remaining British colonies, many of which were following the example of India, which had gained independence in 1947, and were seeking independence themselves.

The major difficulties faced by Churchill were the Mau Mau Rebellion in Kenya and the Malayan Emergency and, having previously stated that he did not intend to preside over the end of empire, he responded to both with direct military action. In both cases the insurgencies were put down, primarily because the rebels did not command support from all sections of society. But although his policies were successful at the time, there was little Churchill could do to prevent either country from an inevitable progress towards independence. This would be achieved in Kenya in 1957 and Malaya in 1963, when the newly-independent country was given the name of Malaysia.

Churchill's other major area of interest was in international relations, particularly those between America and the Soviet Union. He attempted to renew the special relationship he had established with America, flying to Washington four times to meet with President Truman and then with Eisenhower after he was elected President in 1952. One of Churchill's main aims, particularly after Stalin's death in March 1953, was to attempt to persuade the Americans to enter into talks with the Soviet Union with the goal of ending the Cold War and thus reducing the threat of nuclear confrontation. On one occasion, thinking that Eisenhower was willing to meet the Soviets, he approached them without consulting his own Cabinet, causing a rift with Eden who, as Foreign Secretary, should have been involved. But such initiatives did not mean Churchill favoured nuclear disarmament. In June 1954, he was instrumental in the decision that Britain should build its own nuclear bomb, seeing it as both a deterrent and a means of giving Britain a greater say in international affairs.

In June 1953, Churchill suffered another stroke, which affected his speech and caused some paralysis down his left side. The details of his illness were kept from the public and, during the four months he spent convalescing, he was said to be suffering from exhaustion. He returned to public life in October with few visible signs remaining of his health problems but, from this time onwards, he frequently came under pressure to step down from senior figures in the Conservative

Party, particularly Eden, the prime candidate to succeed him.

During 1953, Churchill accepted a knighthood. He had previously declined a peerage because he wanted to remain in the House of Commons and because he did not want his son Randolph, who would have inherited the peerage, to be prevented from pursuing a political career in the Commons. In the same year, he was also awarded the Nobel Prize for Literature, with the citation saying he had been given the prize 'for his mastery of historical and biographical description as well as for brilliant oratory in defending exalted human values'. It is debatable whether Churchill would have been given the prize had the committee making the award been aware that sections of *The Second World War* had, in large part, been the work of the Syndicate.

Churchill told Eden on a number of occasions in 1954 that he was retiring only to change his mind. Finally, in April 1955 and at the age of 80, he stepped down as Prime Minister and was succeeded by Eden, who had waited so long for his chance but was destined to last as Prime Minister only until January 1957 before he was obliged to resign in the aftermath of the Suez Crisis. Churchill was again offered a dukedom by the Queen and again he preferred to remain in the House of Commons, which he did for a further nine years, attending debates and voting but not making any speeches.

The Long Day Closes

After Churchill retired as Prime Minister the decline in his physical and mental powers, which had begun to become apparent towards the end of the war and became more so after his stroke in 1953, steadily got worse. He continued to spend time in the South of France and occupied himself with painting but he was ill more frequently and suffered from periods of depression, the 'black dog' that had accompanied him for much of his life and which he had kept at bay with continuous activity.

One of the last occasions he travelled up to London from Chartwell was on his ninetieth birthday in November 1964, when he acknowledged the crowds gathered in front of his London home in Hyde Park Gate with a characteristic V for Victory sign. By this time, he had suffered further strokes and was largely confined to a wheelchair. During the night of 9 January 1965 he had a final massive stroke and two weeks later, on 24 January, he died without regaining consciousness.

Churchill was given a state funeral, which remains the last such occasion in Britain it was granted to anyone other than a member of the Royal Family. His coffin lay in state in Westminster Hall while hundreds of thousands of people filed past to pay their respects. After three days it was borne on a gun-carriage through the streets of London, which were lined with mourners, to St Paul's Cathedral for the funeral service. It was then taken by river barge and train to the village of Bladon in Oxfordshire where, as his will had requested, Churchill was laid to rest in the family plot, next to his brother Jack and within sight of Blenheim Palace, where he had been born ninety years before.

Great Briton

It is now more than forty years since Churchill died and, in that time, debates have raged over his life and legacy. Like many public figures, he has been subjected to character assassinations and he has also been accused at one time or another of being the architect of almost all the ills of the modern world. Much of the criticism has been a consequence of particular authors pursuing their own (often extreme) political agendas but some of the more reasoned argument has served to cast a clearer light on Churchill than did the unqalified hero worship he often inspired immediately after the Second World War.

While writing his memoirs of the Second World War, Churchill often remarked that he was sure of his place in history because he intended to write it himself. As has been shown by David Reynolds in his brilliant book *In Command of History: Churchill Fighting and Writing the Second World War*, Churchill was determined to present his own version of events, much of which has since become the established story, and he was not above manipulating the facts to cast himself in a better light. Rather than diminish Churchill's achievement, recent research which has clarified some of the issues Churchill himself preferred to obscure, presents a portrait of a real human being, doing the best he could in sometimes impossible circumstances and having to make decisions which affected the lives of millions of people. Perhaps the first challenge to Churchill as the unassailable hero of the war came with the publication of Lord Alanbrooke's diaries in 1957, which had been edited to highlight the frequent disagreements between Churchill and the Chief of the Imperial General Staff and to show that Churchill was not solely responsible for the conduct of the war. It exposed Churchill as often difficult and petulant when he didn't get his own way but, in a telling entry from 1943 in which Alanbrooke vented his frustration with Churchill by writing that he was the most difficult man he had ever worked with, he went on to say, 'but I would not have missed the opportunity of working with him for anything on earth'.

The picture of Churchill that emerges from Alanbrooke's diary, and from the writings of other people who had worked with him during the war, is of a man who often bore the immense responsibility with which he was charged much more heavily than he showed in public. Such descriptions provide a glimpse of the real man which had previously been covered up by the mythology surrounding him, and which Churchill himself made little effort to dispel. Perhaps he aspired to a place in history alongside the great military commanders of the past, such as Wellington and Nelson, who now exist in the public imagination through their deeds but hardly at all as individuals.

Churchill's character flaws lie before us exposed. We know about his impetuosity, belligerence and conceit as well as about all the terrible mistakes he made during his long political career. But, in the end, his reputation surely rests on those months between March 1940 and December 1941 when Britain fought on alone against the tyranny of Nazi Germany. There were moments during this period when he all but dragged the country back from the brink of defeat by the force of his personality alone, inspiring the people of Britain to keep on fighting no matter what the odds. It is difficult to imagine any other British political figure who would have been able to achieve a similar response. For all his obvious faults and mistakes, in those months of adversity he proved himself with words and actions which can only be described as heroic.

Notes

1   Diana, Princess of Wales was a descendant of Charles
    Spencer, the third Earl of Sunderland, making her a distant
    relative of Churchill. She could also trace her ancestry to
    Arabella Churchill, the first Duke of Marlborough's sister,
    through Henrietta FitzJames, one of the four illegitimate
    children Arabella had with King James II.
2   In his biography of Winston Churchill, Roy Jenkins points
    out the irony that Lord Randolph is mostly remembered as
    a father, a responsibility he largely neglected in favour of his
    political career, which is now widely regarded as a failure.
3   The reports Churchill wrote while in Africa were later
    published as *My African Journey*.
4   Up until 1964, when the Admiralty was incorporated into
    the Ministry of Defence, the First Lord of the Admiralty was
    the head of the Royal Navy, traditionally a civilian from the
    Government of the day who held a seat in the Cabinet. The
    professional head of the navy was and remains the First Sea
    Lord.
5   The *Enchantress* is usually described as a yacht, but this
    doesn't really give an indication of the size of the ship. It had
    a displacement of 3,800 tons and a crew of 192.
6   In order to conceal the nature of the research being carried
    out to develop landships, documents referred to the work as
    being done to construct 'water tanks for Russia', leading to

all those who were involved in the project calling the resulting vehicles 'tanks'.

7   In Australia and New Zealand 25 April is now marked as ANZAC Day, and the name Gallipoli has a similar resonance in those countries to that of the Somme in Britain or Verdun in France.

8   The territory that is now Iraq had been three separate Ottoman provinces before the British mandate, centred on the cities of Mosul in the north, Baghdad in the middle and Basra in the south. The differences between the Kurds, Sunni Muslims and Shia Muslims in these three regions were as apparent then as they remain today. The Hasemite monarchy established by Faisal in Iraq lasted until 1958, when it was overthrown in a *coup d'etat* by the Iraqi Army, while King Abdullah II, the great grandson of King Abdullah I, remains the constitutional monarch of the Hasemite Kingdom of Jordan, as the country is now officially called.

9   The Treaty Ports were Berehaven and Queenstown in County Cork and Lough Swilly in Donegal. They were returned to Ireland in 1938, much to Churchill's annoyance. During the Second World War these ports, had they remained under British control, could have been used to refuel Royal Navy ships during the Battle of the Atlantic, but to do so after they had been returned to Ireland would have been breaking Irish neutrality.

10 The activities of the code-breakers at Bletchley Park and the resulting Ultra intelligence remained an official secret in Britain until 1974.

11 Britain owed America about $35 billion at the end of the war, equivalent to about $500 billion today. The debt was finally paid off at the end of 2006.

12 The relevant lines from the St Crispin's Day speech in Shakespeare's Henry V are:
From this day to the ending of the world,
But we in it shall be remember'd,
We few, we happy few, we band of brothers.

13 The Cabinet War Rooms are now open to the public and include a museum devoted to Churchill's life. Blenheim Palace and Chartwell are also open to the public.

14 As caretaker Prime Minister, Churchill was consulted by President Truman over the dropping of the atomic bombs on Hiroshima and Nagasaki. According to an agreement between Britain and America, the use of atomic weapons required the approval of both countries, which Churchill gave on 4 July 1945, although he was no longer in office when the bombs were actually dropped in August.

Bibliography

Addison, Paul, *Churchill: The Unexpected Hero*, Oxford: OUP, 2005

Cannadine, David and Quinault, Roland (eds), *Winston Churchill in the Twenty-First Century*, Cambridge: CUP, 2004

Churchill, Randolph S., *Winston S. Churchill Vol 2: Young States-man 1901–1914*, London: Heinemann, 1967

Churchill, Winston S., *My Early Life*, London: Thornton Butterworth, 1931

Churchill, Winston S., *The Second World War*, 6 vols, London: Cassell, 1948–1954

Gilbert, Martin, *Churchill: A Life*, London: Heinemann, 1991

Gilbert, Martin, *Winston Churchill's War Leadership*, New York: Vintage, 2004

Gilbert, Martin, *Winston S. Churchill Vols 3 to 7: v3, 1914–1916; v4, 1917–1922; v5, 1922–1933; v6, Finest Hour 1939–1941; v7, Road to Victory 1941–1945*; London: Heinemann, 1971–1986

Hastings, Max, *Overlord: D-Day and the Battle for Normandy 1944*, London: Michael Joseph, 1984

Jenkins, Roy, *Churchill*, London: Macmillan, 2001

Reynolds, David, *In Command of History: Churchill Fighting and Writing the Second World War*, Harmondsworth: Allen Lane, 2004

Wasserstein, Bernard, *Barbarism and Civilisation: A History of Europe in Our Time*, Oxford: OUP, 2007

Index